ANNYEONG?

A New Learning Paradigm rich in Culture and Stories

KOREAN!

1

ANNYEONG? KOREAN! _ Volume 1

First published in 2025 by Hello Korean Inc.
© 2025 Jieun Kiaer, Hyun Mi Kim and Nicola Fraschini
Manuscript Review: **Lee. Inhye**
English Proofreading: **Gabriel Sparta**
Published by **Hur. Dae woo**
Marketing by **Kim. Cheol kyu / Hwang. Hyun kyung**
Designed by **Lee. Seung mi**
Character Design by **Lee. Jae yeop**

ISBN 979-11-988638-2-9 (13700)
eBook ISBN 979-11-988638-3-6 (15700)
Printed and bound in Republic of Korea by Hello Printec

AUTHORS

Jieun Kiaer

Prof Jieun Kiaer is the YBM KF Professor of Korean Linguistics at the University of Oxford. She also serves as a Korean Consultant for the Oxford English Dictionary and is recognized as a leading expert in Korean linguistics and Hallyu (Korean Wave) studies. Prof Kiaer holds a PhD in Linguistics from King's College London, as well as an MA in Linguistics and a BA in Child and Family Studies from Seoul National University. Her innovative approaches to language learning include fandom language learning, AI-driven digital linguistics, and storytelling methods that integrate culture and personal interests.

Hyun Mi Kim

Hyun Mi Kim has taught Korean to students in Canada, South Korea, the United States, and now Australia. Through her various teaching roles, she learned what students want by listening and connecting their interests with curriculum requirements. This dedication earned her the Citations for Outstanding Contributions to Student Learning from the University of Western Australia. Her rich experience enabled her to develop the Korean curriculum for the Western Australia Department of Education. Additionally, students' questions inspired her to co-author three books, including *Mission Accomplished Korean 1 & 2* (Hawoo, 2022/2023) and *Korean Conversation Gambits* (Routledge, 2024). She holds a B.A. in education and an M.A. in Korean culture from Ewha Womans University. Her cultural studies background leads her to believe that engaging students in Korean culture through language strengthens their connection to Korean society and enhances understanding. She feels that learning languages builds connections and friendships, cultivating hope for a brighter future.

Nicola Fraschini

Nicola Fraschini is a Senior Lecturer at the University of Melbourne, where he is Convener of the Korean Studies program and director of the Global Korea Research Hub. His research interests are the psychology of language teaching and learning and Q methodology. He is co-author of the textbooks *Mission Accomplished: Korean 1 & 2* (Hawoo, 2022/2023), and co-editor of *Advancing Language Research through Q Methodology* (Multilingual Matters, 2024) and *Innovative Methods in Korean Language Teaching* (Routledge, 2025). In 2024, he was awarded from the Republic of Korea the Prime Minister's citation for his work supporting the Korean language.

FOREWORD

The Korean language is quickly gaining global popularity, largely due to the cultural phenomenon known as Hallyu, or the Korean Wave. However, interest in Korea now extends beyond K-pop fans and those enchanted by K-dramas. Professor Jieun Kiaer, who launched *Annyeong? Hangeul!*, is now joined by Hyunmi Kim and Nicola Fraschini in the series *Annyeong? Korean!*. The authors share a common goal of celebrating and enhancing intercultural connections while promoting the learning of the Korean language and culture in an inclusive and accessible manner that supports a long-term learning experience.

People around the world are learning Korean to connect more deeply with its vibrant culture and broaden their perspectives. Traditional textbooks, however, often lack the real-life, practical experiences that make modern Korean culture so engaging, focusing more on rules than on everyday language. *Annyeong? Korean!* was created to fill this gap, bringing learners closer to the language and culture in a way that feels immediate, relevant, and engaging.

In this series, you'll find real-life situations, relatable characters, and story-driven lessons designed to immerse you in contemporary Korea. *Annyeong? Korean!* connects you to the everyday language and culture you experience in Korea, from daily interactions to K-dramas and media. This approach fosters a deeper understanding, allowing you to feel connected to the people and places behind the language.

Annyeong? Korean! supports sustainable language learning with a pathway aligned to the International Standard Curriculum for the Korean language and the Common European Framework of Reference (CEFR), blending practical skills with cultural insights that grow with you. Each of the 10 books builds upon core language skills, pragmatics, and situational learning, helping you navigate social nuances and interact naturally in real-world settings.

Through iconic Korean locations-such as cozy hanok guesthouses in Hongdae, the vibrant Han River Park, popular beauty stores like Olive Young, and the thrilling atmosphere of LOL Park for esports-*Annyeong? Korean!* brings the language to life, offering an experience that feels real and close. This series is designed to be inclusive and accessible, whether you're a student, a professional, a parent, or a lifelong learner, in a classroom or through self-study.

So, are you ready to start this journey? 준비되었나요? Let's dive into the language and culture of Korea together and make every moment of learning feel connected, meaningful, and inspiring.

The authors

CONTENT

STRUCTURE

Unit	Title	Vocabulary and Expressions	Grammar	Dialogue
1	Guest house	Accommodation and lodging	이에요/예요; 은/는	Tao checks in at Sumbisori Guest house
2	Welcome to Korea	Nationality and personal information; public transportation	이/가; ...이/가 아니에요	Priya and Tao introduce each other
3	Convenience store: 24 hours is not enough	Everyday objects and goods	이, 그, 저; ...이/가 있다; ...에 있다	Sarang talks to a customer at the convenience store
4	It's Olive Young again, today!	Everyday objects and goods	...에 가다; ...에서 오다	Haru asks Sophia to buy some items at Olive Young
5	The Han River Park and ramyeon	Food	–(으)세요; 시간 + 에	Sophia and Sam go to a food stall at the Han River Park
6	#Seoulmuseumsuggestion	Museums and public venues	–아요/어요; 을/를; ...에서 + 동사	Caroline and Gabriel talk about visiting a museum
7	Cinnamon punch in iced americano	Drinks; traffic and directions	안; (으)로	Tao and Priya discuss about coffee and beverages
8	League of Legends Park	Hobbies	–았어요/었어요; 못	Sophia and Tao talk the activities they did during the past weekend
9	Train to Busan	Travel booking and reservations	–고 싶다; –(으)ㄹ까요?	Sam contacts a travel agency to change his booking
10	Famous restaurants near the mountains	Leisure activities	형용사 –(으)ㄴ; –(으)러 가다	Umid, Gabriel, Maduka and Priya make an arrangement for the weekend

Reading	Listening	Activity	Culture
Guest house advertisement	Airport coach payment instructions	Self introduction	Seoul's living spaces
Public transport information	Bus information	Jobs and professions	President Yoon Suk Yeol-Defined Age: A New Chapter for Koreans?
Convenience store flyer	Buying goods at a convenience store	Shopping at a convenience store	Solo dining and driver's restaurants: The culture of 24-hour work in Korea
Enquiry email and reply	Shopping at Olive Young	Online shopping	Do you know GRWM? Dive into K-beauty with "get ready with me"
Instructions to cook ramyeon	Using the transportation card	Ordering at a street food stall	Dalgona: From Squid Game to the Oxford English Dictionary
Museum brochure	Museum guide instructions	Preparing a flyer for a museum exhibition	Ganada song
Korean map app	Ordering at a Korean traditional tea house	Providing street directions	A coffee-loving Korean: 405 cups a year!
Blog entry	Telling friends about past experiences	Writing a travel diary	Eating samgyeopsal while playing e-games?
KORAIL website announcement	KTX speaker annuncement	Plan a trip in Korea and explain your plan to your friend	Busan International Film Festival
Blog entry	Discussing with friends about where to eat	Organise a food trip in Korea	From ajeossi to trendsetter: The rise of the hiking clothes fashion

UNIT STRUCTURE

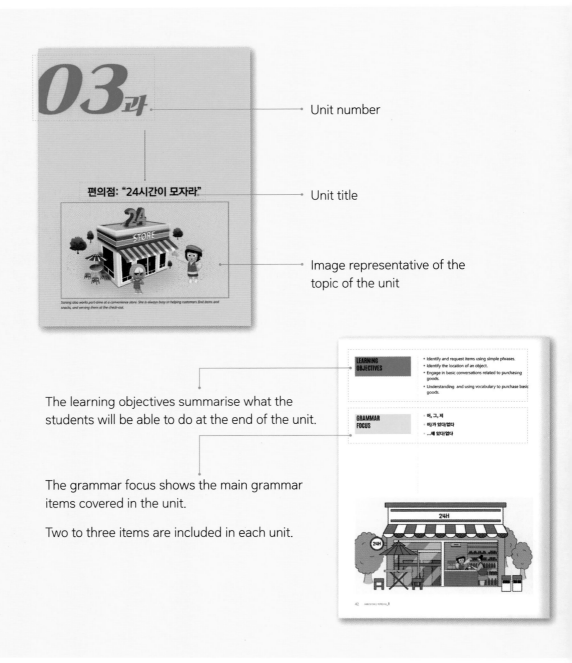

03과

Unit number

편의점: "24시간이 모자라"

Unit title

Image representative of the topic of the unit

The learning objectives summarise what the students will be able to do at the end of the unit.

The grammar focus shows the main grammar items covered in the unit.

Two to three items are included in each unit.

LEARNING OBJECTIVES
- Identify and request items using simple phrases.
- Identify the location of an object.
- Engage in basic conversations related to purchasing goods.
- Understanding and using vocabulary to purchase basic goods.

GRAMMAR FOCUS
- 이, 그, 저
- 이/가 있다/없다
- ...에 있다/없다

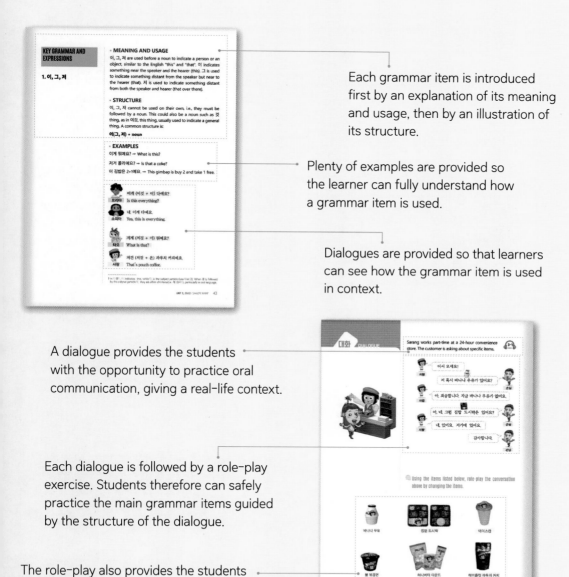

Each grammar item is introduced first by an explanation of its meaning and usage, then by an illustration of its structure.

Plenty of examples are provided so the learner can fully understand how a grammar item is used.

Dialogues are provided so that learners can see how the grammar item is used in context.

A dialogue provides the students with the opportunity to practice oral communication, giving a real-life context.

Each dialogue is followed by a role-play exercise. Students therefore can safely practice the main grammar items guided by the structure of the dialogue.

The role-play also provides the students with new vocabulary to learn.

UNIT STRUCTURE

Reading activities are structured into three parts. In the pre-reading activity, students practice vocabulary and expressions to fully understand the reading.

In the reading activity students approach the main material. The material for the reading activities has a different format in every unit, spanning from advertisements, to blogs, to flyers to short narratives, in order to expose students to a range of contexts where languages is used in distinct ways.

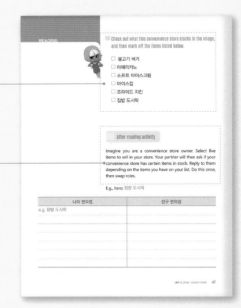

After each reading, the students can check their understanding of the content through quizzes and open ended questions.

A follow-up reading activity provides the opportunity to expand the communicative setting, by using the content learned in either a written or an oral activity.

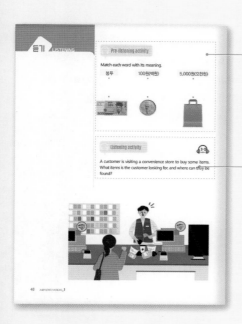

Each listening activity is introduced with an exercise that helps learners become familiar with the vocabulary and expressions featured in the main listening.

The main listening is always introduced by a listening question, i.e., what the learners should focus on while listening to the recording.

At the end of the listening activity, the students will find an exercise they can use to check their comprehension.

At the end of the main listening activity, the students have the opportunity to practice the language learned in the unit in a real-life situation.

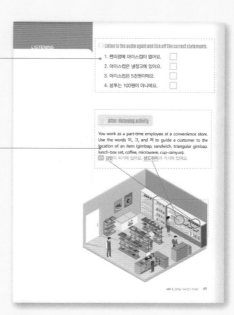

UNIT STRUCTURE

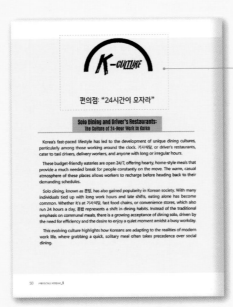

A K-culture corner introduces the students to an aspect of contemporary Korean culture and society mentioned in the unit.

A K-media corner provides suggestions to the students for films, dramas, and fiction works through which they can observe and experience the main cultural aspects included in the unit. Through these suggestions, students can also maximise their language exposure.

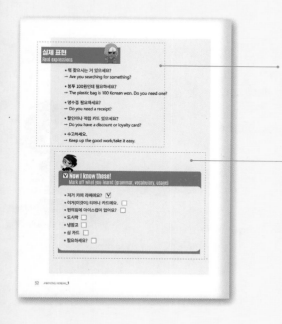

The students can also get used to real expressions that they may hear in Korea.

At the end of each unit, the students can reflect on their learning through a reflective sheet.

CHARACTERS

Sarang(사랑) Sarang has British-Korean background, and she is the manager of Sumbisori's Guest house, located near Hongdae station. She also works part-time at a convenience store.

Haru(하루)

Haru is a Japanese student interested in Korean dramas and K-pop. He is in Seoul to learn Korean.

Priya(프리야) Priya is from Indonesia. In her country, she is a Korean language teacher.

Tao(타오)

Tao is from China. He likes Korean food and he is into e-sports.

Caroline(캐롤라인) Caroline is from the US. She is professor of history at university, and she is in Korea to learn more about Korean culture and history.

Maduka(마두카) Maduka is a university student from Nigeria. He is traveling to Korea for pleasure.

Sophia(소피아)

Sophia is from France. She is passionate about sport, and she is a YouTuber.

Sam(샘) Sam is from Australia. He loves cooking and loves Australian football and cricket.

Gabriel(가브리엘)

Gabriel is from Canada. He studies architecture, and he is interested in Korean traditional houses. His grand-father participated in the Korean War.

Umid(우미드) Umid is from Uzbekistan and has Korean ancestry. He is a professional graphic designer.

Jina Ssaem(지나쌤)

Jina Ssaem is a Korean teacher in Annyeong? Korean! Series

01 과

게스트하우스

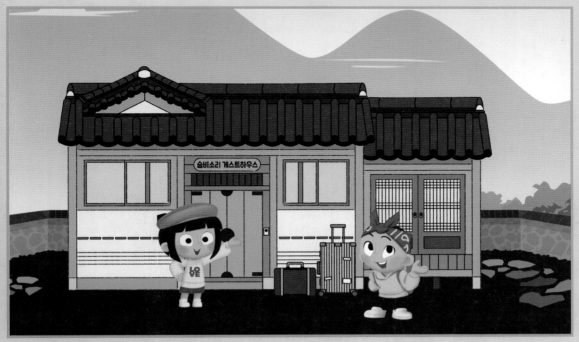

Sarang manages a cozy hanok-style guesthouse in Hongdae, Seoul. Sarang helps Tao with checking in, then together with they head to the airport to pick up a new friend coming to the guest house.

LEARNING OBJECTIVES

- Introduce yourself and greet others.
- Understand payment options for public transportation.
- Understand and use vocabulary related to accommodations and lodging.

GRAMMAR FOCUS

- 이에요/예요
- 은/는

KEY GRAMMAR AND EXPRESSIONS

1. 이에요/예요

• MEANING AND USAGE

이에요/예요 is used to indicate identity (e.g., this person is Sarang), a state (e.g., this building is Sumbisori Guest house), or a fact (e.g., this is my phone). Korean generally employs a subject + object + predicate format, differing from the common English structure of subject + predicate + object. For this reason, 이에요/예요 is used at the end of the sentence. In English, it corresponds to the verb 'to be'.

• STRUCTURE

이에요/예요 is attached to a noun. Use 이에요 after nouns ending in a consonant and 예요 after those ending in a vowel.

• EXAMPLES

타오

이름이 뭐예요?
What is your name?

사랑

저는 사랑이에요. 이분은 캐롤라인 씨예요.
I am Sarang, this (person) is Caroline.

타오

캐롤라인 씨, 직업이 뭐예요?
Caroline, what is your job?

캐롤라인

교수예요. 타오 씨는요?
I am a professor. What about you?

타오

저는 대학생이에요.
I am a (university) student.

2. 은/는

• MEANING AND USAGE

은/는 is a topic particle. In Korean, particles are attached mostly to nouns to indicate a grammatical function, and as such have no translation in English. 은/는 indicates the topic of the sentence, or "what is being talked about", a known piece of information, something which has already been mentioned before. Therefore, the usage of 은/는 depends on the context.

• STRUCTURE

은 is attached to nouns ending with a consonant, and 는 to nouns ending with a vowel.

• EXAMPLES

타오

이름이 뭐예요?
What is your name?

사랑

저는 사랑이에요. 이분은 캐롤라인 씨예요. 캐롤라인 씨는 미국 사람이에요.
I am Sarang, this (person) is Caroline. She is American.

우미드

치콜이 뭐예요?
What is Chikol?

가브리엘

치콜은 치킨하고 콜라예요.
This is the Chikol set. Chikol is chicken and Coke.

A new guest is checking in at Sumbisori Guest house.

사랑: 어서 오세요!

타오: 여기가 숨비소리[1] 게스트하우스예요?

사랑: 네, 맞아요! 제 이름은 사랑이에요. 매니저예요.

타오: 아, 저는 왕타오예요. 중국 사람이에요.

사랑: 만나서 반가워요.

타오: 네, 반가워요. 지금 체크인 괜찮아요?

사랑: 네, 지금 괜찮아요. 여권 주세요.[2]

Look at the name tags below and use them to role-play the dialogue with your partner. Then, fill out your name tag with your name and nationality.

| 이름: 왕타오 | 이름: 아라이 하루 | 이름: 김 우미드 | 이름: | 이름: |
| 나라: 중국 | 나라: 일본 | 나라: 우즈베키스탄 | 나라: | 나라: |

1 In the dialect of Jeju Island, 숨비소리 refers to the breathing sound of a traditional Korean female diver, known as haenyeo.
2 Real expression is 여권 좀 보여주시겠어요?

📖 **Pre-reading activity**

Match the pictures to the Korean words below.

게스트 하우스	화장실	와이파이	온돌	에어컨

1.
2.
3.
4.
5.

📖 **Reading activity**

Check out Sumbisori's Guest house homepage. What options can you find at there Sumbisori Guest house?

숨비소리 게스트하우스

| 인사말 | 공간구성도 | 예약 | 오시는길 | Sign in |

안녕하세요? 숨비소리 게스트하우스예요.

▶게스트하우스 이름: 숨비소리
▶게스트하우스 지역: 홍대
▶시간: 체크인 오후 3시/체크아웃 오전 11시
▶외국어: 영어, 일본어, 중국어
▶옵션:
　🚽 개인 화장실　🧴 욕실 용품
　📺 냉난방　🧤 부엌(조리 기구)
　📺 TV　((•)) WIFI/인터넷

Read carefully the guest house homepage information, then check off the items that indicate the correct information.

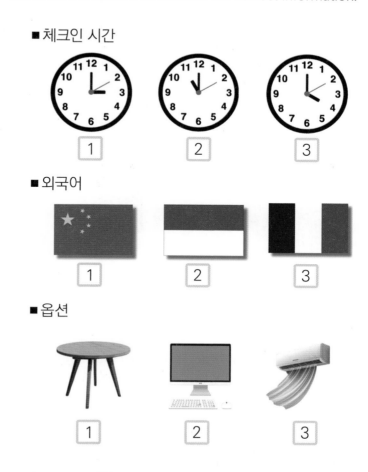

■체크인 시간

1   2   3

■외국어

1   2   3

■옵션

1   2   3

After-reading activity

Fill out the missing syllable of the following words.

• 와이____이 (WiFi)

• 체크____웃 (Check out)

• 에어____ (Air Conditioner)

• 중____어 (Chinese language)

• ____장실 (Toilet)

• 온____ (Korean traditional heating system)

• 안녕____세요? (Hello!)

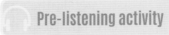 Pre-listening activity

Match the pictures to the correct words/expressions.

| 현금 | 여기 찍으세요. | 신용 카드 |

Listening activity

Tao and Sarang are heading to the airport bus stop to pick up their friend from the guest house who is visiting Korea. The bus has just arrived. Which terminal are they heading to, and what payment method will be used for the bus?

Listen to the conversation between Tao, Sarang and the bus driver. Then, select any words or expressions you hear in the conversation.

Words/Expressions		Words/Expressions	
신용카드	✓	에어컨	
안녕하세요?		현금	
나라		여기에 찍으세요.	
이름		와이파이	

After-listening activity

Create a self-introduction to share with other guesthouse residents, taking inspiration from Maduka's example. Make sure to incorporate a greeting, your nationality, and your profession.

안녕하세요? 저는 마두카예요.
저는 나이지리아 사람이에요.
제 집은 라고스예요.
저는 대학생이에요.
만나서 반가워요.

"게스트하우스"

Seoul's Living Spaces

Seoul offers a wide range of accommodation options, especially for students and young people preparing for their future.

Popular choices include 고시원 (tiny study rooms), one-room apartments, and 반지하 (semi-basement) units. 고시원, originally meant for those studying for civil service exams in areas like 노량진, provide basic, affordable living spaces, making them popular for budget-conscious students facing intense competition.

One-room apartments offer more space and privacy but can be pricey, especially in areas like 강남. 반지하 units, made famous by the film *Parasite*, are often cramped and damp but serve as cheaper alternatives in Seoul's competitive housing market.

Despite the many apartment buildings in the city, Seoul's high population density and soaring housing prices contrast sharply with rural areas, where housing is plentiful but underused.

This imbalance highlights Korea's diverse yet challenging living options, with urban areas struggling with high demand and rural homes remaining empty.

K-MEDIA CORNER

Sumbisori is a cozy Hanok style guest house in Hongdae, Seoul and is where the stories in **Annyeong? Korean!** start. These guesthouses, common in cities, offer shared spaces, simple yet inviting rooms, and a sense of community, making them perfect for students, young professionals, and those looking for affordable housing.

In **Doona!**, the guesthouse is a place where characters connect, reflecting how these spaces foster community. **Reply 1988** shows close bonds in shared living during the 1980s, while **Start-Up** highlights young entrepreneurs supporting each other in modern co-living. **Hotel Del Luna** adds a magical twist, with its hotel bringing together wandering souls, emphasising connections beyond life.

 How do shared living spaces in K-dramas reflect changing housing trends and community values in Korea?

 What cultural insights can we gain about Korean society from the portrayal of guest houses and communal living?

[이미지 출처: 네이버/유튜브]

▶ 웹툰: 꽃미남 게스트하우스 IN 북촌

- 성함이 어떻게 되세요?
→ What is your name? (This is a polite way of asking for a name)

- 여권 좀 보여주시겠어요?
→ May I see your passport?

- 어느 터미널로 가세요?
→ Which terminal are you going to?

- 어느 호텔로 가세요?
→ Which hotel are you going to?

- 어디에서 내리실 거예요?
→ Which bus stop will you get off at? (Lit. Where will you get off?)

- 여기에 카드를 대세요.
→ Please place your card here.

- 카드를 다시 대 주세요.
→ Please place your card (here) again.

☑ Now I know these!
Mark off what you learnt (grammar, vocabulary, usage)

- 게스트하우스 ☑
- 만나서 반가워요. ☐
- 여권 주세요. ☐
- 현금 ☐
- 신용 카드 ☐
- 여기 찍으세요. ☐

02과

웰컴 투 코리아

WELCOME TO KOREA

In this chapter, Sarang and her friends navigate their way from Incheon Airport to the guesthouse, getting their first taste of Korea's energy as they find their way through bustling streets and public transport.

LEARNING OBJECTIVES

- Ask and answer questions related to personal information.
- Inquire about a location or about public transportation.
- Understand and use vocabulary related to nationality and other personal information.

GRAMMAR FOCUS

- 이/가
- 이/가 아니에요

KEY GRAMMAR AND EXPRESSIONS

1. 이/가

• MEANING AND USAGE

이/가 is a particle attached to a noun to indicate the subject of the sentence. As such, it depends on the grammatical structure of the sentence (and not on the context, as in 은/는 seen in unit 1).

• STRUCTURE

이 is attached to nouns ending with a consonant and 가 to nouns ending with a vowel.

• EXAMPLES

타오

이름이 뭐예요?
What is your name?

사랑

저는 사랑이에요.
I am Sarang.

하루

이분이 누구예요?
Who's this person?

타오

이분은 캐롤라인 씨예요.
This person is Caroline.

타오

마두카 씨가 어느 나라 사람이에요?
Which country is Maduka from?

샘

나이지리아 사람이에요.
He is from Nigeria.

소피아

이 티머니 카드가 누구 거예요?
Whose T-Money card is this?

가브리엘

제 거예요.
It's mine.

2. 이/가 아니에요

• MEANING AND USAGE

아니에요 is the negative counterpart of 이에요/예요, therefore it is used to say that "something is not...". In sentences where 아니에요 is used, 이/가 is usually attached to the noun indicating the person or the object that "is not".

• STRUCTURE

The typical structure of a sentence where 아니에요 is used is:

A은/는 + B이/가 아니에요. A is not B.

• EXAMPLES

사랑 씨는 인도네시아 사람이 아니에요.
→ Sarang is not Indonesian.

이 사람은 제 친구가 아니에요.
→ This person is not my friend.

그건 제 아이디어가 아니에요.
→ That is not my idea.

샘
이거 플랫화이트예요?
Is this a flat white?

프리야
아니요. (이건) 플랫화이트가 아니에요. 카페라떼예요.
No, it's not. This is a café latte.

하루
오늘이 소피아 씨 생일이에요?
Is today your birthday, Sophia?

소피아
오늘은 제 생일이 아니에요. 내일이에요.
Today isn't my birthday; tomorrow is.

Newcomers to the Sumbisori Guest house introduce themselves to each other.

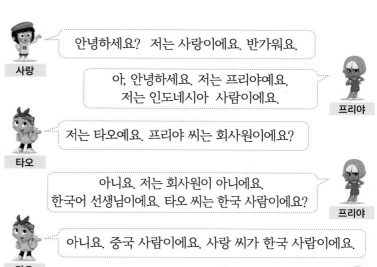

사랑: 안녕하세요? 저는 사랑이에요. 반가워요.

프리야: 아, 안녕하세요. 저는 프리야예요. 저는 인도네시아 사람이에요.

타오: 저는 타오예요. 프리야 씨는 회사원이에요?

프리야: 아니요. 저는 회사원이 아니에요. 한국어 선생님이에요. 타오 씨는 한국 사람이에요?

타오: 아니요. 중국 사람이에요. 사랑 씨가 한국 사람이에요.

사랑: 네. 그런데 저는 British-Korean이에요.

Look at the examples below and use them to role-play the dialogue with your partner. Change Priya's script to match the other person's nationality and occupation.

	프리야	인도네시아	한국어 선생님
	마두카	나이지리아	대학생
	소피아	프랑스	유튜버
	우미드	우즈베키스탄	그래픽 디자이너

Pre-reading activity

Sophia just arrived at Incheon airport.
What are the transportation options to central Seoul and Sumbisori Guest house?

Reading activity

Sophia is looking at the limousine bus lines at Incheon Airport. Which bus route does she need to take to reach Hongdae Station (홍대입구)?

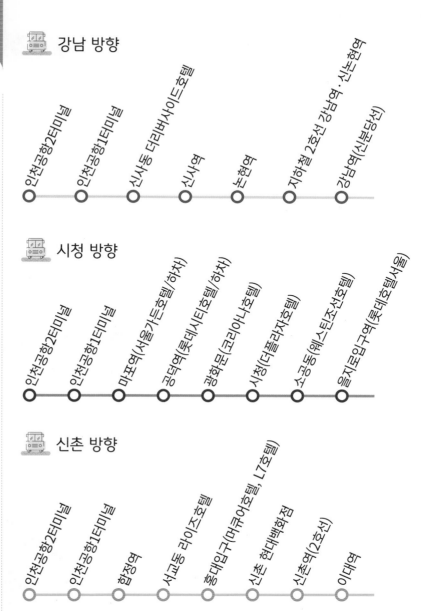

🚌 강남 방향

인천공항2터미널 ─ 인천공항1터미널 ─ 신사동 더리버사이드호텔 ─ 신사역 ─ 논현역 ─ 지하철 2호선 강남역 · 신논현역 ─ 강남역(신분당선)

🚌 시청 방향

인천공항2터미널 ─ 인천공항1터미널 ─ 마포역(서울가든호텔/하차) ─ 공덕역(롯데시티호텔/하차) ─ 광화문(코리아나호텔) ─ 시청(더플라자호텔) ─ 소공동(웨스틴조선호텔) ─ 을지로입구역(롯데호텔서울)

🚌 신촌 방향

인천공항2터미널 ─ 인천공항1터미널 ─ 합정역 ─ 서교동 라이즈호텔 ─ 홍대입구(머큐어호텔, L7호텔) ─ 신촌 현대백화점 ─ 신촌역(2호선) ─ 이대역

📖 **After-reading activity**

You have booked your accommodation at the following places. Which airport coach do you need to take among the above bus routes?

더플라자 호텔	머큐어 호텔
웨스틴 조선(서울) 호텔	더리버사이드 호텔

 Pre-listening activity

 2-2

Listen to the audio file and then fill out the blanks.

1. Passenger: 여기가 시청이에요?

   Bus driver: 아니요. 시청_____. 여기는
   광화문이에요.

2. _____에서 내리세요.[1]

3. _____정류장은 뉴서울 호텔이에요.

 2-3

Listening activity

Umid took the airport bus to get to his accommodation. Listen to the conversation between Umid and the bus driver. Where does Umid get off the bus?

Answer: _____

---

1 "내리세요" means "please get off." This is a polite request expression

After-listening activity

Guessing my partner's job in a word search!

- Form groups of three to work on the word search puzzle together. Inside the puzzle, you'll find a list of job titles hidden.

- After you find all the words, look up what the jobs mean and choose your favourite one in secret. Everyone will take turns asking about each other's jobs to find out. For example, you can ask, "Are you an influencer? (인플루언서 예요?)"

- Each person has three chances to ask questions. Answers can only be "Yes, I am ..." or "No, I am not ..."

Word search puzzle!								
관	러	프	언	경	원	예	듀	술
머	언	로	화	팜	서	회	듀	경
농	어	듀	농	언	머	사	플	찰
듀	학	서	러	이	가	원	디	관
디	자	플	게	술	어	이	자	부
경	인	로	예	원	영	이	너	게
이	프	서	영	화	배	우	회	관
스	마	트	팜	농	부	찰	듀	회
어	듀	너	농	경	디	자	이	너

직업 Occupation
경찰관
디자이너
스마트팜 농부
언어학자
영화배우
예술가
인플러언서
프로게이머
프로듀서
회사원

"웰컴 투 코리아"

President Yoon Suk Yeol-Defined Age:
A New Chapter for Koreans?

In 2023, President Yoon Suk Yeol redefined Korea's age system, simplifying a tradition that caused confusion for decades. Previously, Koreans had two ages: the "Korean age," starting at one from birth, and the "international age," counting from zero.

This made people feel one or two years older than they actually were. The old age system wasn't just a numbers game; it deeply influenced daily interactions.

In Korea, age determines how you speak—using 반말 (casual speech) with younger people and 존댓말 (polite speech) with elders. This affects friendships, school, and work dynamics, making age crucial in social settings.

Yoon's law instantly made everyone a year younger, aligning with global standards. However, old habits die hard, and many still use the traditional age system, leading to awkward moments and continued confusion.

This reform shows that while laws can change, cultural norms are often much harder to shift!

K-MEDIA CORNER

Korean dramas often use speech styles like 반말 (casual speech) and 존댓말(polite speech) to show relationships, respect, and social dynamics. These styles change as characters grow closer, especially in romantic scenes, where formal speech turns informal, reflecting their deepening connection.

In military dramas like *Descendants of the Sun, D.P.*, and *Crash Landing on You*, speech styles are influenced by rank and age, showcasing the hierarchy within the military. *Crash Landing on You* also highlights North Korean speech rules, showing how strict formalities shape interactions. In *Bloodhounds*, characters' speech reflects their age, background, and social ties, adding depth to their relationships.

These shifts in language offer viewers a deeper look into the characters' evolving relationships and make the drama feel more authentic and true to Korean culture.

 How do speech styles like 반말 and 존댓말 highlight social hierarchies in Korean culture?

 What do these speech dynamics reveal about relationships and power in Korean society?

[이미지 출처: 네이버/유튜브]

▶ Extra reading: the book 아드님 진지 드세요 helps children understand honorifics and appreciate the personal importance of language.

- 누가 벨 누르셨어요?
→ Who pressed the bus bell?

- 어디까지 가세요?
→ What is your destination?

- 여기 아니에요. 다음 (정류장)에서 내리세요.
→ It's not here; please get off at the next stop.

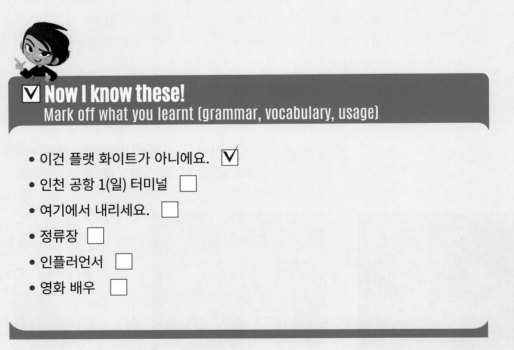

☑ Now I know these!
Mark off what you learnt (grammar, vocabulary, usage)

- 이건 플랫 화이트가 아니에요. ☑
- 인천 공항 1(일) 터미널 ☐
- 여기에서 내리세요. ☐
- 정류장 ☐
- 인플러언서 ☐
- 영화 배우 ☐

03과

편의점: "24시간이 모자라"

Sarang also works part-time at a convenience store. She is always busy in helping customers find items and snacks, and serving them at the check-out.

LEARNING OBJECTIVES

- Identify and request items using simple phrases.
- Identify the location of an object.
- Engage in basic conversations related to purchasing goods.
- Understanding and using vocabulary to purchase basic goods.

GRAMMAR FOCUS

- **이, 그, 저**
- **이/가 있다/없다**
- **...에 있다/없다**

KEY GRAMMAR AND EXPRESSIONS

1. 이, 그, 저

• MEANING AND USAGE

이, 그, 저 are used before a noun to indicate a person or an object, similar to the English "this" and "that". 이 indicates something near the speaker and the hearer (this). 그 is used to indicate something distant from the speaker but near to the hearer (that). 저 is used to indicate something distant from both the speaker and hearer (that over there).

• STRUCTURE

이, 그, 저 cannot be used on their own, i.e., they must be followed by a noun. This could also be a noun such as 것 thing, as in 이것, this thing, usually used to indicate a general thing. A common structure is:

이(그, 저) + noun

• EXAMPLES

이게 뭐예요? ➝ What is this?

저거 콜라예요? ➝ Is that a coke?

이 김밥은 2+1예요. ➝ This gimbap is buy 2 and take 1 free.

 프리야
이게 (이것 + 이)[1] 다예요?
Is this everything?

 소피아
네. 이게 다예요.
Yes, this is everything.

 타오
저게 (저것 + 이) 뭐예요?
What is that?

 사랑
저건 (저것 + 은) 파우치 커피예요.
That's pouch coffee.

---

1 In 이것이, 이 indicates this, while 이 is the subject particle (see Unit 2). When 것 is followed by the subject particle 이, they are often shortened in 게 (것+이), particularly in oral language.

2. ...이/가 있다

• MEANING AND USAGE

Depending on the context, 있다/없다 can be used to express that somebody has something (first meaning) or that somebody or something is somewhere (second meaning). In the examples below, 있다 means "to have (something)", and 없다 means "to not have" something.

• STRUCTURE

When 있다/없다 has the meaning of "to have (not) something", it generally follows this structure:

A은/는(or 이/가) B이/가 있어요. A has B.

• EXAMPLES

타오 씨는 공항 버스 티켓이 있어요.
→ Tao has a ticket for the airport coach.

소피아 씨는 한국 심 카드가 없어요.
→ Sophia doesn't have a Korean SIM card.

3. ...에 있다/없다

• MEANING AND USAGE

...에 있다/없다 is used to indicate that somebody (or something) is somewhere.

• STRUCTURE

A이/가(은/는) + place + 에 있다/없다 **A is/is not somewhere.**

• EXAMPLES

바나나 우유가 편의점에 있어요.
→ Banana milk is at the convenience store.

타오 씨가 서울에 있어요.
→ Tao is in Seoul.

대화 DIALOGUE

Sarang works part-time at a 24-hour convenience store. The customer is asking about specific items.

사랑: 어서 오세요!

손님: 저 혹시 바나나 우유가 있어요?

사랑: 아, 죄송합니다. 지금 바나나 우유가 없어요.

손님: 아, 네. 그럼 집밥 도시락은 있어요?

사랑: 네, 있어요. 저기에 있어요.

손님: 감사합니다.

Using the items listed below, role-play the conversation above by changing the items.

바나나 우유

집밥 도시락

아이스컵

불 볶음면

허니버터 아몬드

헤이즐럿 파우치 커피

 Pre-reading activity

What items do you usually buy at a convenience store or at a mart? Please provide the items in Korean using the web dictionary. (*https://dict.naver.com/* or scan the QR code.)

Reading activity

Look at the image below and answer the question: What does this convenience store offer?

24시간 편의점
FOOD & COFFEE

불고기버거 4.0	떡꼬치 2.0	프라이드 치킨 2.0
BULGOGI BURGER	TTEOK KKOCHI	FRIED CHICKEN
아메리카노 2.0	카페라떼 2.5	소프트 아이스크림 2.0 SOLD OUT
AMERICANO	CAFE LATTE	SOFT ICECREAM

📖 Check out what this convenience store stocks in the image, and then mark off the items listed below.

☐ 불고기 버거

☐ 아메리카노

☐ 소프트 아이스크림

☐ 아이스컵

☐ 프라이드 치킨

☐ 집밥 도시락

📖 After-reading activity

Imagine you are a convenience store owner. Select five items to sell in your store. Your partner will then ask if your convenience store has certain items in stock. Reply to them depending on the items you have on your list. Do this once, then swap roles.

E.g., item: 집밥 도시락

나의 편의점	친구 편의점
e.g. 집밥 도시락	

Pre-listening activity

Match each word with its meaning.

봉투   100원(백원)   5,000원(오천원)

Listening activity

A customer is visiting a convenience store to buy some items. What items is the customer looking for, and where can they be found?

🎧 Listen to the audio again and tick off the correct statements.

1. 편의점에 아이스컵이 없어요. ☐
2. 아이스컵은 냉장고에 있어요. ☐
3. 아이스컵은 5천원이에요. ☐
4. 봉투는 100원이 아니에요. ☐

💬 **After-listening activity**

You work as a part-time employee at a convenience store. Use the words 이, 그, and 저 to guide a customer to the location of an item (gimbap, sandwich, triangular gimbap, lunch-box set, coffee, microwave, cup-ramyun).

ex 김밥이 저기에 있어요. 샌드위치가 거기에 있어요.

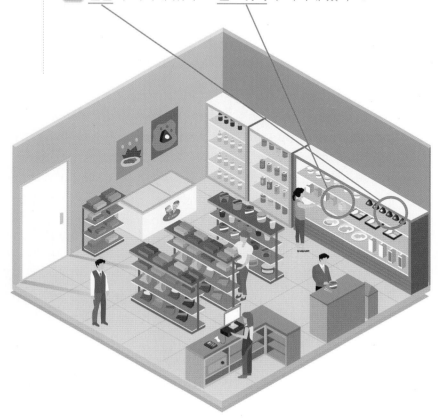

편의점: "24시간이 모자라"

Solo Dining and Driver's Restaurants:
The Culture of 24-Hour Work in Korea

Korea's fast-paced lifestyle has led to the development of unique dining cultures, particularly among those working around the clock. 기사식당, or driver's restaurants, cater to taxi drivers, delivery workers, and anyone with long or irregular hours.

These budget-friendly eateries are open 24/7, offering hearty, home-style meals that provide a much needed break for people constantly on the move. The warm, casual atmosphere of these places allows workers to recharge before heading back to their demanding schedules.

Solo dining, known as 혼밥, has also gained popularity in Korean society. With many individuals tied up with long work hours and late shifts, eating alone has become common. Whether it's at 기사식당, fast food chains, or convenience stores, which also run 24 hours a day, 혼밥 represents a shift in dining habits. Instead of the traditional emphasis on communal meals, there is a growing acceptance of dining solo, driven by the need for efficiency and the desire to enjoy a quiet moment amidst a busy workday.

This evolving culture highlights how Koreans are adapting to the realities of modern work life, where grabbing a quick, solitary meal often takes precedence over social dining.

K-MEDIA CORNER

Korean dramas and novels often showcase the nonstop world of 24-hour convenience stores, mirroring the hustle and resilience of modern Korean society.

Backstreet Rookie dives into the lives of a convenience store owner and his lively part-time employee, capturing the ups and downs of working late-night shifts and the unexpected friendships formed along the way.

Similarly, the novel ***Uncanny Convenience Store*** explores the hidden lives of those connected to a store, highlighting how these places become sanctuaries in a fast-paced world.

 How do convenience stores represent the 24-hour lifestyle in Korea?

 What do these spaces tell us about community roles and social interactions in Korean urban life?

[이미지 출처: 네이버/유튜브]

한국을 넘어 세계를 사로잡은 K-힐링소설의 대표작
오직 독자의 선택과 입소문이 만든 경이로운 밀리언셀러

★★★★★ | ★★★★★ | ★★★★★ | ★★★★★
주요 서점 80주 연속 | 전 세계 18개국 | 전국 37개 도시 | 2022 공공도서관
종합 베스트 Top 10 | 판권 수출 | 올해의 책 | 최다 대출 도서

- 뭐 찾으시는 거 있으세요?
→ Are you searching for something?

- 봉투 100원인데 필요하세요?
→ The plastic bag is 100 Korean won. Do you need one?

- 영수증 필요하세요?
→ Do you need a receipt?

- 할인이나 적립 카드 있으세요?
→ Do you have a discount or loyalty card?

- 수고하세요.
→ Keep up the good work/take it easy.

☑ Now I know these!
Mark off what you learnt (grammar, vocabulary, usage)

- 저거 카페 라떼예요? ☑
- 이게(이것이) 티머니 카드예요. ☐
- 편의점에 아이스컵이 없어요? ☐
- 도시락 ☐
- 냉장고 ☐
- 심 카드 ☐
- 필요하세요? ☐

오늘도 올리브영

Sophia and Haru discuss about items they need to buy at Olive Young, before Sophia heads to the shop. Meanwhile Maduka, a new friend from Nigeria, sends an email to Sarang to book a room and ask about transportation from the airport.

LEARNING OBJECTIVES

- Use numbers to indicate a quantity of items. [1]
- Enquiry about items you want to purchase.
- Understand and use vocabulary related to common everyday life objects.

GRAMMAR FOCUS

- …에 가다
- …에서 오다

---

1 See the appendix for the number p.138.

KEY GRAMMAR AND EXPRESSIONS

1. …에 가다

• MEANING AND USAGE

…에 가요 means "to go to". 에 is a particle attached to a place to indicate direction; 가요 is the present tense of the verb "to go".

• STRUCTURE

A 이/가 (or 은/는) + place에 가요. A goes to place.

• EXAMPLES

타오 씨가 올리브영에 가요.
→ Tao goes to Olive Young.

캐롤라인 선생님이 한국에 가요.
→ Professor Caroline goes to Korea.

하루 소피아 씨, 어디에 가요?
Where are you headed?

소피아 산에 가요.
I'm heading to the mountains.

2. ···에서 오다

• MEANING AND USAGE

···**에서 와요** means "to come from". 에서 is a particle attached to a place to indicate origin; 와요 is the present tense of the verb "to come".

• STRUCTURE

A 이/가 (or 은/는) + place에서 와요. A comes from "place".

• EXAMPLES

마두카 씨가 나이지리아에서 와요.
→ Maduka comes from Nigeria.

하루 씨는 공항에서 와요.
→ Haru comes from the airport.

Sophia is heading to the Olive Young store in Myeongdong to buy a toothbrush set. Haru asks her to pick something up for him as well.

하루: 어? 소피아 씨, 어디에 가요?

소피아: 아, 지금 명동 올리브영에 가요.

하루: 왜요?

소피아: 칫솔하고 치약이 없어요. 그리고 지금 올영 세일[2]이에요.

하루: 그래요? 그럼 남자 면도 크림 하나하고 면도기 세 개만 사다 주세요[3]

소피아: 네. 알겠어요.

하루: 고마워요!

Look at the items and quantities below. Use them to roleplay the dialogue with your partner.

2개   3개   1병   4통   5개   10장

---

2 "올영 세일" refers to the sale period at Olive Young stores.

3 "사다 주세요" is a Korean phrase that translates to "Please buy (something) for me." It is a polite expression.

READING

📖 **Pre-reading activity**

What kind of options are you looking for when you search for accommodation? Look at the icons below, and with the help of your teacher, write what they indicate in Korean.

1. 🖥 TV _____
2. ▭ 에어컨 _____
3. 🗄 _____
4. ▣ _____
5. 🚽 _____
6. 🖊 _____
7. ((ᵠ)) _____

📖 **Reading activity**

Maduka is about to go to Korea. He is looking for accommodation and is writing an email to Sarang. What is Maduka asking about?

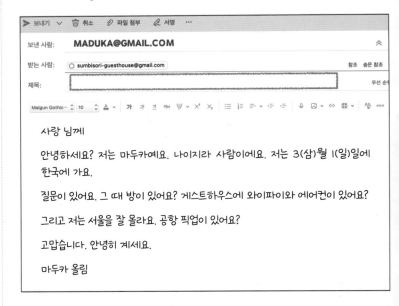

📖 **Read Maduka's email and answer the questions.**

1. 마두카 씨는 어느 나라 사람이에요?

2. 마두카 씨는 언제 한국에 가요?

3. 마두카 씨는 사랑 씨한테 무슨 질문을 해요? (세 개)

After-reading activity

This is Sarang's reply to Maduka's queries.

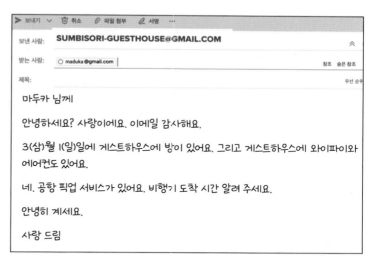

> 보내기 ∨   🗑 취소   📎 파일 첨부   ✍ 서명   …

보낸 사람: **SUMBISORI-GUESTHOUSE@GMAIL.COM**   ☆

받는 사람: ○ maduka @gmail.com | 참조 숨은 참조

제목: 우선 순위

마두카 님께

안녕하세요? 사랑이에요. 이메일 감사해요.

3(삼)월 1(일)일에 게스트하우스에 방이 있어요. 그리고 게스트하우스에 와이파이와 에어컨도 있어요.

네, 공항 픽업 서비스가 있어요. 비행기 도착 시간 알려 주세요.

안녕히 계세요.

사랑 드림

📖 Review the statements below and choose any that are correct.

1. 숨비소리 게스트하우스에 3(삼)월 1(일)일에 방이 있어요. ☐

2. 숨비소리 게스트하우스에 와이파이와 TV가 있어요. ☐

3. 숨비소리 게스트하우스에 공항 픽업 서비스가 없어요. ☐

Check the initial email from Maduka. Then, think about how to create an effective subject line for this email. Finally, write down the subject line for Maduka. Also, what inquiries would you Maduka if you were searching for a guesthouse in Korea now?

- Maduka's subject line:

_____

_____

- Your inquiries about the guest house:

_____

_____

듣기 LISTENING

 Pre-listening activity

Listen to the audio file and then fill out the blanks.

1. Customer: 립밤_____개 _____있어요?
   Staff: 네. 잠시만요. 여기에 있어요.
2. 면도기는 _____개 있어요.

 Listening activity

Sophia has arrived at the Olive Young store. What kind of items is she looking for, and how many?

🎧 Pick the correct items and quantity that Sophia is looking for.

면도기 2개 + 왁스 3개	면도기 1개 + 립밤 3개
면도기 3개 + 립밤 3개	선크림 3개 + 립밤 3개

After-listening activity-conversation

https://global.oliveyoung.com/

Visit the Olive Young online store. Explore the website, add a few items you need to your shopping cart, and then share the items and quantities with your partners.

제 카트에는 비타민 1통하고
파운데이션 리필 3개가
있어요.

"오늘도 올리브영"

GRWM, or "Get Ready With Me," has become a viral trend on TikTok, especially in the K-Beauty scene. It's more than just a morning routine; it's a captivating experience where influencers share their makeup, skincare, and fashion tips in engaging videos.

K-Beauty is celebrated for its emphasis on a multi-step skincare routine, including products like 에센스 (essence), 토너 (toner), and 앰플 (ampoule), which are essential for achieving that radiant, dewy glow.

GRWM videos are not just tutorials—they're a peek into the latest K-Beauty trends, from the popular 쿠션 파운데이션 (cushion foundation) to the 마스크팩 (sheet mask) craze. These clips offer viewers a chance to learn about the importance of cleansing, moisturizing, and applying sunscreen, key steps in K-Beauty's approach to flawless skin.

For Korean learners, GRWM videos on TikTok are also a fun way to pick up everyday Korean phrases like 피부 관리 for "skincare" and 메이크업 for "makeup."

K-Beauty's influence goes beyond the products; it's a blend of beauty, culture, and language, making learning an interactive and stylish experience. So, get ready, glow up, and learn Korean with K-Beauty!

K-MEDIA CORNER

True Beauty and *My ID is Gangnam Beauty* explore the pressure to meet beauty standards in Korean society. *True Beauty* follows Lim Ju-Kyung, who uses makeup to change her appearance after being bullied, highlighting the emotional impact of societal expectations.

My ID is Gangnam Beauty focuses on Kang Mi-rae, who undergoes plastic surgery to escape her past but faces new judgments about her "artificial" beauty. Both dramas critique the obsession with appearance, emphasizing the challenges of fitting in and the journey towards self-acceptance in a beauty-conscious culture.

How does True *Beauty* and *My ID is Gangnam Beauty* show the impact of beauty standards on young people?

What do these dramas teach us about self-acceptance and looking beyond appearances?

[이미지 출처: 네이버]

▶ Extra reading: 27 Of The Best K-Beauty Products Worth The Hype, Sarah Y. Wu.
https://www.forbes.com/sites/sarahwu/2024/06/03/27-of-the-best-k-beauty-products-worth-the-hype/

- 지금 명동 올리브영에 가는데 혹시 필요한 거 있어요?
→ I'm heading to Myeongdong Olive Young; do you need anything?

- 비행기 도착 시간 알려 주세요.
→ Please inform me of the arrival time of your flight.

- 3월 1일에 방을 예약하고 싶은데 예약이 가능한지 궁금합니다.
→ I want to book a room for March 1 and wanted to check its availability.

☑ Now I know these!
Mark off what you learnt (grammar, vocabulary, usage)

- 소피아 씨, 어디에 가요? ☑
- 면도기 ☐
- 세 개만 사다 주세요. ☐
- 마두카 씨가 나이지리아에서 와요. ☐
- 저는 서울을 잘 몰라요. ☐
- 한국어를 알아요. ☐
- 잠시만요. ☐

05과

한강 공원과 라면

Caroline helps out Sophia in taking the bus to go to the Han River Park. At the park, Sophia meets up with Sam, and the two enjoy a sunny day cooking ramyeon.

LEARNING OBJECTIVES

- Order food and drinks using simple sentences.
- Make polite requests.
- Learn to use the Sino-Korean[1] series of numbers.
- Understand and use food-related vocabulary.

GRAMMAR FOCUS

- -(으)세요
- 시간 + 에

1 See the appendix for the number. p.139

KEY GRAMMAR AND EXPRESSIONS

1. -(으)세요

• MEANING AND USAGE

-(으)세요 is attached to the base of verbs to indicate a polite request or to politely invite somebody to do something (a polite order).

• STRUCTURE

Verb base ending with a consonant + -으세요
Verb base ending with a vowel + -세요

• EXAMPLES

(버스에서) 손잡이를 꽉 잡으세요.
→ Hold on to the handles (on the bus).

참깨라면 한 개 주세요.
→ Please give me a bowl of sesame ramyeon.

선생님: 여러분, 지금부터 대화문을 읽으세요.
→ Teacher: Everyone, please read the dialogue now.

학생: 네.
→ Students: Okay.

프리야   캐롤라인 선생님, 커피 한 잔 하세요.
Professor Caroline, please have a cup of coffee.

캐롤라인   고마워요, 프리야 씨!
Thank you, Priya!

2. 시간 + 에

• MEANING AND USAGE

에 is a particle used after expressions of time. However, it is not used after the following words as they are exceptions: **어제** yesterday, **오늘** today, **내일** tomorrow, **지금** now.

• STRUCTURE

Expression of time + 에

• EXAMPLES

(저는) 오전 9시에 학교에 가요.
→ I go to school at 9am.

마두카 씨는 3월 1일에 나이지리아에서 와요.
→ Maduka will come from Nigeria on March 1st.

 타오 씨가 언제 롤파크 PC방에 가요?
Tao, when do you go to the LoL (League of Legends)
하루 Park internet café?

 보통 저녁에 롤파크 PC방에 가요.
Tao usually goes to the LoL (League of Legends)
소피아 Park internet café in the evening.

 소피아 씨가 오늘 롤파크 굿즈 숍에 가요.
Today Sophia goes to the LoL (League of Legends)
하루 Park's merchandise shop.

[이미지 출처: 네이버]

Sophia and Sam visited the Han River Park and are ordering ramyeon from a street stall.

소피아: 짜파게티 1개 얼마예요?

점원: 4,000원이에요.

샘: 신라면 한 개하고 물은 얼마예요?

점원: 신라면은 4,000원, 물은 1,000원이에요.

샘: 그럼 짜파게티 1개, 신라면 1개, 물 2병 주세요.

점원: 여기 있어요. 10,000원이에요.

소피아: 감사합니다.

…

소피아: 짜파게티 라면이 맛있어.

샘: 오우, 신라면도 맛있어. 그런데 조금 매워.

💬 Look at the items below and use them to role-play the dialogue with your partner, changing the item, price, and quantity.

 물 `800 원`

 계란 `3,000원`

 담요 `4,000원`

 돗자리 `1,200 원`

 바나나 우유 `1,000 원`

읽기 READING

Pre-reading activity

What do you need to cook ramyeon? Review the images below and write down the names listed in the boxes.

스프	계란	건더기	면	물	젓가락

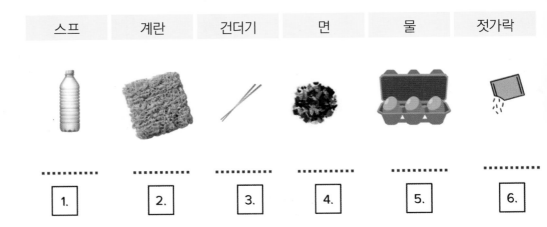

1. _____

2. _____

3. _____

4. _____

5. _____

6. _____

Reading activity

These are the instructions for preparing instant ramyeon. How do you prepare ramyeon?

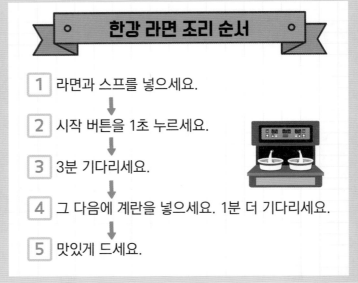

한강 라면 조리 순서

1. 라면과 스프를 넣으세요.

2. 시작 버튼을 1초 누르세요.

3. 3분 기다리세요.

4. 그 다음에 계란을 넣으세요. 1분 더 기다리세요.

5. 맛있게 드세요.

📖 The following step is missing from the instructions above. After which step would you add it?

'삐–' 소리가 나요. 그럼 끝이에요.

📖 **After-reading activity**

Look at the images below and arrange them in the correct order to prepare ramyeon. Then, give instructions to your friend on how to prepare ramyeon.

A. 1 ....

B. ....

C. ....

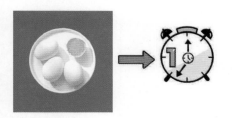

D. ....

E. ....

F. ....

LISTENING

 **Pre-listening activity**

How do you pay for public transportation in your country? With cash, card, transport card, phone, or ticket? Listen to the audio file, fill out the blanks, and guess what is used in Korea to pay for public transportation.

1. 사랑: 기사님, 3명이에요!

   Bus driver: 잠깐만 _____. 지금 _____를 대세요.

2. 캐롤라인: 한국에서 카드 _____으로 3명이 탈 수 있어요.²

   소피아: 알겠어요.

 **Listening activity**

Sophia is heading to Banpo Han River Park this weekend, but she realised at the bus stop that she doesn't have a transport card. Caroline is also at the bus stop, heading in the same direction. Listen to the following conversation between Sophia and Caroline and find out what item Sophia forgot. What did Caroline say to the bus driver?

🎧 After listening to the conversation again, put the following sentences in order as you would hear them on the bus.

↓

↓

"지금 카드를 대세요."

"잠깐만요. 기다리세요."

"기사님, 2명이에요."

2 탈 수 있어요 means one "can take" (a form of transportation).

After-listening activity-conversation

You may find these items at an outdoor stall on the Han River. Do you know how to name all of these? Use the items below and do a role-play with your partner, with one of you being the seller and the other a customer. Don't forget to use appropriate expressions. Start with " _____주세요."

If you are buying, don't forget:

> 1. ···주세요.
> 2. 얼마예요?
> 3. 감사합니다.

If you are selling, don't forget:

> 몇 개 드릴까요?
> 매운 거? 안 매운 거?
> 젓가락 필요해요?

한강공원과 라면

Dalgona:
From Squid Game to the Oxford English Dictionary

달고나, a crunchy and sweet Korean candy, is now included in the Oxford English Dictionary.

This nostalgic treat became globally famous through the Netflix hit *Squid Game*, where players had to carefully cut out shapes—like stars or umbrellas—from the candy using a needle without breaking it.

Traditionally, 달고나 was made by melting sugar, stirring in baking soda, and then flattening the mixture into discs with fun shapes pressed into the center. It was sold near primary schools at 문방구 (stationery shops) and considered simple 불량식품 (junk food).

During the COVID-19 lockdowns, 달고나 made a big comeback with the viral 달고나 coffee challenge on TikTok, where people whipped sugar and instant coffee into a fluffy drink.

Alongside other Korean street foods like 떡볶이 (spicy rice cakes), 호떡 (sweet pancakes), and 붕어빵 (fish-shaped bread), 달고나 shows how these humble treats capture global attention. From a childhood snack to a worldwide sensation, 달고나 proves that even the simplest foods can make the biggest impact.

K-MEDIA CORNER

Korean food culture is celebrated worldwide, with dishes like 김치 (kimchi), 불고기 (bulgogi), 비빔밥 (bibimbap), and 떡볶이 (tteokbokki) recognised in the Oxford English Dictionary. *I Want to Die but I Want to Eat Tteokbokki* by Baek Sehee highlights food's emotional comfort.

Dramas like *Let's Eat* showcase the joy of shared meals, while *Little Forest* depicts healing through cooking with fresh ingredients. Han Kang's *The Vegetarian* explores food as personal rebellion. Historical dramas like *Mr. Sunshine* use dishes like 빙수 (shaved ice) to reflect tradition and modernity.

 How do Korean dramas and films *like Let's Eat and Little Forest* depict the connection between food and emotional healing? Why do you think food plays such a significant role in these stories?

 In what ways do works like *The Vegetarian* and *Mr. Sunshine* use food to explore cultural identity and personal transformation? What do these narratives reveal about the broader cultural significance of food in Korean society?

[이미지 출처: 네이버/유튜브]

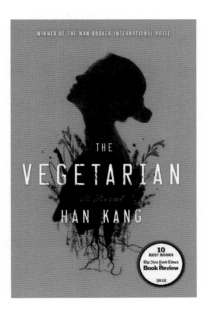

- 한강 라면 조리 방법 → How to cook Han River Ramyeon

1. 전용기에 라면과 스프를 넣은 후 조리기에 올려 주세요.
   → Place the ramen noodles and soup in the ramyeon bowl, then insert it into the cooker.
2. 조리 시작 버튼을 1초 정도 살짝 눌러 주세요.
   → Press the start cooking button for approximately 1 second.
3. 물이 자동으로 공급되어 조리를 시작합니다. (물이 뜨거워요.)
   → Hot water will automatically be supplied to begin cooking.
4. 계란은 1분 정도 시간이 남았을 때 넣어 주세요.
   → When there's about 1 minute left, add the egg.
5. 조리 중 천천히 라면을 저어준 뒤 삐 소리와 램프 불이 꺼지면 천천히 꺼내 주세요.
   → Gently stir the ramyeon during cooking, and when you hear the beep and see the light go out, carefully remove it.

☑ Now I know these!
Mark off what you learnt (grammar, vocabulary, usage)

- (버스에서) 손잡이를 꽉 잡으세요. ☑
- 교통 카드 ☐
- 맛있어. ☐
- 신라면은 4,000원, 물은 1,000원이에요. ☐
- 매워. ☐
- 지금 카드를 대세요. ☐
- 카드 1장으로 3명이 버스 탈 수 있어요. ☐

06과

#서울박물관추천

Sarang suggests Gabriel to visit the War Memorial of Korea. Gabriel and Caroline decide to visit the Memorial together, and do not miss the opportunity to learn about Korean history guided by a friendly tour guide.

LEARNING OBJECTIVES

- Ask for directions and recommendations.
- Discuss schedules and activities.
- Use basic verbs in the present tense to describe actions.

GRAMMAR FOCUS

- -아요/어요
- 을/를
- ...에서 + 동사

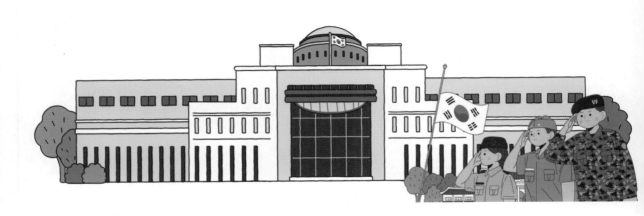

KEY GRAMMAR AND EXPRESSIONS

1. -아요/어요

• MEANING AND USAGE

-아요/어요 is attached to the base of verbs and descriptive verbs (roughly equivalent to adjectives) to indicate the present tense at an informal but polite level. This is the speech level most used in everyday life.

• STRUCTURE

-아요 is attached to verb bases containing ㅏ or ㅗ, while -어요 is attached to verb bases containing other vowels. 하다 becomes 해요.

받다→ 받 + 아요 → 받아요
가다→ 가 + 아요 → 가요
오다→ 오 + 아요 → 와요
먹다 → 먹 + 어요 → 먹어요
마시다 → 마시 + 어요 → 마셔요
주다 → 주우 + 어요 → 줘요
하다 → 하 + 여요 → 해요

• EXAMPLES

소피아 씨는 국립중앙박물관에서 무슨 선물을 사요?
→ What gift does Sophia buy at the National Museum?

우미드 씨가 박물관에서 사진을 찍어요.
→ Umid takes photos in the museum.

참! 전쟁기념관에서 뭐 해요?
→ What do you do at the War Memorial of Korea?

[이미지 출처: 네이버_국립중앙박물관]

2. 을/를

• MEANING AND USAGE

을/를 is a particle used to indicate the grammatical object of a (transitive) verb.

• STRUCTURE

을 is attached to nouns ending with a consonant, 를 is attached to nouns ending with a vowel.

• EXAMPLES

하루 씨가 오늘 전쟁기념관을 구경해요.
→ Today Haru tours the War Memorial of Korea.

캐롤라인 선생님이 한국 드라마를 봐요.
→ Professor Caroline watches Korean dramas.

3. 에서 + 동사

• MEANING AND USAGE

에서 is a particle attached to places used to indicate that a certain action happens or is conducted in that place.

• STRUCTURE

place + 에서 + verb indicating action

• EXAMPLES

캐롤라인 선생님이 전쟁기념관에서 사진을 많이 찍어요.
→ Professor Caroline takes lots of photos at the War Memorial of Korea.

타오 씨가 숨비소리 게스트하우스에서 숙박해요.
→ Tao stays at Sumbisori Guest house.

Caroline is asking Gabriel to recommend a museum in Korea.

캐롤라인

가브리엘 씨, 박물관 좀 추천해 주세요.

용산에 전쟁기념관이 있어요. 거기 어때요?

가브리엘

캐롤라인

오, 좋아요! 전쟁기념관에서 뭐 해요?

아, 거기서 전시회를 구경해요.

가브리엘

캐롤라인

와~ 너무 좋아요!!
저는 한국 역사 공부를 좋아해요.

💬 Look at the sentences below and use them to engage in a dialogue with your partner, replacing the colour-coded phrases with the prompts provided.

전시회를 구경하다

한국 전쟁 이야기를 듣다

한국 역사를 배우다

Fill in the blanks with the words provided in the note.

```
휴관
주말
주중
무료
```

1. 전쟁기념관은 관람료가 _____ 예요.
2. 박물관은 보통 월요일이 _____ 이에요.
3. 우미드 씨는 _____ 에는 바빠요. 월요일부터 금요일까지 그래픽 디자인 회사에서 일해요.
4. 우미드 씨는 _____ 에는 쉬어요. 토요일하고 일요일에 캠핑을 가요.

📖 Reading activity

The following brochure provides information about visiting the War Memorial of Korea in Seoul. Explain what kind of information is illustrated in the brochure.

시간	9:30~18:00
관람료	무료
휴관	매주 월요일, 1월 1일, 설날, 추석
투어 가이드	주중: 오전 10시, 오후 2시 주말: 오전 10시 30분, 2시 30분
투어 가이드 장소	2층 한국전쟁실

전쟁기념관 안내
가이드 투어

The War Memorial of Korea
홈페이지 언어: 한국어, 영어, 일본어, 중국어
교통: 지하철 - 삼각지역 (4호선, 6호선),
　　　버스 - 110A, 110B, 740, 421

📖 **Check off the statement if it is correct.**

1. 전쟁기념관은 오전 9시 30분부터 오후 6시까지 열어요. ☐

2. 전쟁기념관은 관람료가 없어요. ☐

3. 전쟁기념관은 매주 일요일이 휴관이에요. ☐

4. 투어 가이드 시간은 주중하고 주말 시간이 같아요. ☐

5. 투어 가이드 선생님을 2층 한국전쟁실에서 만나요. ☐

📖 **After-reading activity**

Identify the museums or art galleries in Korea that interest you. Next, research and complete the flyer.

_____
안내
가이드 투어

| 시간 |
| 관람료 |
| 휴관 |
| 투어 가이드 |
| 투어 가이드 장소 |

박물관/미술관 이름:
홈페이지 언어:
교통:

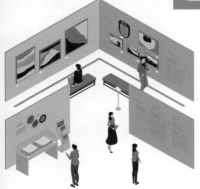

Pre-listening activity

Refer to the map on the left to identify the location's name, then link the sentence describing the locations.

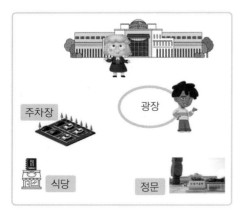

전시관 •	• 선생님: "저쪽에 있어요."
광장 •	• 선생님: "식당 근처에 있어요."
주차장 •	• 선생님: "이쪽에 있어요."
식당 •	• 선생님: "정문 뒤에 있어요."

Listening activity

The tour guide explains the War Memorial map before starting the exhibition tour. Which locations and facilities did she mention?

A. Note the locations and facilities introduced by the tour guide.

E.g., 메인 전시관

B. Listen again to review the guide's brief overview and mark any correct statements.

1. 가이드 선생님은 전쟁기념관을 설명해요. ☐
2. 평화 광장은 정문 옆에 있어요. ☐
3. 주차장 근처에 식당과 카페가 많아요. ☐
4. 화장실은 메인 전시관 근처에 있어요. ☐
5. 기념품은 메인 전시관 2층에서 팔아요. ☐

After-listening activity

Imagine you are organising a museum exhibition. Start by completing the details in the text below, and then provide your visitors with information regarding the exhibition's title, opening hours, admission fees, location, tour guides' availability, and available on-site facilities. Look at the given sample and make sure to change the information underlined with those of your exhibition.

Example:
전시회 제목은 "전통 미술, 현대 기술을 만나다"예요. 전시회는 10월 10일부터 내년 12월 15일까지 열어요. 시간은 오전 10시부터 오후 5시까지예요. 매주 화요일에 쉬어요. 그리고 메인 전시관에 휠체어와 엘리베이터가 있어요. 휠체어가 필요해요? 그럼 1층 안내 데스크에 말하세요.
수어 서비스도 있어요. 그래서 수어로 전시물을 설명해요.

The theme of the exhibition is "Traditional Art Meets Modern Technology." It will run from October 10 to December 15 of next year, open daily from 10 a.m. to 5 p.m., except for Tuesdays. The main exhibition hall is accessible with wheelchairs and elevators. If you require a wheelchair, please inform the information desk on the first floor. Additionally, they offer a sign language service to explain the exhibits.

전시회 제목은 "_____"예요. 전시회는 _____부터 내년 _____까지 열어요. 시간은 _____부터 _____까지예요. 매주 _____에 쉬어요. 그리고 메인 전시관에 _____가 있어요. _____가 필요해요? 그럼 1층 안내 데스크에 말하세요. _____서비스도 있어요. 그래서 _____.

#한글박물관추천

Ganada song (가나다송)

A new song called Ganada Song has been created to make learning the Korean alphabet, Hangeul, easier for global audiences, similar to how The ABC Song helps English learners.

Composed by Kim Hyung-suk, with lyrics by Oxford University professor Jieun Kiaer, one of the authors of *Annyeong? Korean!*, the song blends a Beatles-inspired vibe with K-pop elements.

Available on platforms like Spotify, Apple Music, and YouTube, it is designed as a fun and accessible tool for Korean language education worldwide.

Extra video about the Korean alphabet, 한글, from the National Hangeul Museum.

K-MEDIA CORNER

Korean history and war are key themes in films that capture the struggles of ordinary people. *Ode to My Father* follows a man's dedication to his family amid events like the Korean and Vietnam Wars, highlighting the resilience of Koreans through turbulent times.

Welcome to Dongmakgol offers a whimsical take on the Korean War, showing North and South Korean soldiers finding common ground in a remote village.

Operation Chromite dramatizes the Battle of Incheon, emphasizing the strategic collaboration between South Korean forces and UN allies. The American film *Devotion* tells the story of Jesse Brown, the U.S. Navy's first Black aviator, spotlighting friendship and sacrifice during the Korean War.

 How do movies like *Ode to My Father* and *Welcome to Dongmakgol* show the personal impact of the Korean War on people's lives?

 What do *Operation Chromite* and *Devotion* teach us about the role of international forces during the Korean War?

[이미지 출처: 네이버/유튜브]

실제 표현
Real expressions

- 괜찮은/가 볼 만한 전시회 좀 추천해 주세요!
→ Please suggest some notable exhibits worth visiting.

- 기념관 전시관 입구 앞에 평화 광장이 있습니다.
→ Peace Square is at the entrance of the Memorial Exhibition Hall.

- 기념품은 메인 전시관 입구 오른편에 있는 기념품점에서 사실 수 있습니다.
→ The gift shop, located to the right of the main entrance, offers souvenirs.

☑ Now I know these!
Mark off what you learnt (grammar, vocabulary, usage)

- 가이드 선생님이 전쟁기념관을 설명해요. ☑
- 저는 한국 역사 공부를 좋아해요. ☐
- 관람료 ☐
- 휴관 ☐
- 주중에는 바빠요. 그런데 주말에는 시간이 많아요. ☐
- 기념품은 메인 전시관 1층에서 팔아요. ☐

07과

수정과 IN 아·아

Priya and Tao talk about their preferred beverages, then together with Haru they set to explore Korea's coffee culture and traditional Korean beverages.

LEARNING OBJECTIVES

- Ask and provide directions.
- Ask and express personal preferences.
- Indicate the position of objects.
- Understand and use vocabulary related to traffic and street directions.

GRAMMAR FOCUS

- 안
- (으)로

KEY GRAMMAR AND EXPRESSIONS

1. 안

2. (으)로

• MEANING AND USAGE

안 is used before verbs to indicate a negative meaning.

• STRUCTURE

안 is used before verbs; however, when the verb is a compound of noun + 해요, 안 is placed after the noun and before 해요.

• EXAMPLES

프리야 씨는 저녁에는 커피를 안 마셔요.
→ Priya doesn't drink coffee in the evening.

타오 씨는 게임을 안 좋아해요.
→ Tao doesn't like to video games.

가브리엘 씨는 월요일부터 금요일까지 바다 수영해요. 그런데 주말에는 바다 수영 안 해요.
→ Gabriel swims in the ocean Monday through Friday but doesn't swim on weekends.

• MEANING AND USAGE

(으)로 is a particle used to indicate a direction toward a place.

• STRUCTURE

(으)로 is attached to a noun ending with a consonant, and 로 to a noun ending with a vowel.

• EXAMPLES

우미드

화장실이 어디예요?
Where is the restroom?

사랑

저기서 오른쪽으로 가세요.
Go right over there.

2. (으)로

택시 기사

어디로 갈까요?
Where should we go?

택시 손님

삼성 병원으로 가 주세요.
Please go to the Samsung hospital.

우미드 씨가 평화광장에서 친구를 기다려요. 그런데 갑자기 비가 많이 와요. 그리고 우미드 씨는 우산이 없어요. 그래서 우미드 씨가 메인 전시관 안으로 들어가요. 거기서 친구를 기다려요.

→ Umid is waiting for his friend in the Peace Square. But suddenly it is raining hard. And Umid does not have an umbrella. So Umid goes inside the main exhibition hall. There, he waits for his friend.

프리야

캐롤라인 씨, '집으로'는 영어로 무슨 뜻이에요?
Caroline, what does the movie "집으로" mean in English?

캐롤라인

아, 그건 "The Way Home"이에요. 그 영화 진짜 좋아요! 꼭 보세요.
Oh, it's "The Way Home." I love that movie! You should see it.

[이미지 출처: 네이버]

As Tao enters the room, Priya is about to have a cup of coffee in the guest house kitchen.

타오: 프리야 씨, 안녕하세요?

프리야: 안녕하세요? 타오 씨, 커피 마셔요?

타오: 아니요. 저는 커피 안 마셔요. 차를 마셔요. 프리야 씨는 커피 좋아해요?

프리야: 네, 저는 아·아[1]를 너무 좋아해요. 그래서 저는 아·아를 하루에 5잔 마셔요.

타오: 와~! 안 추워요?

프리야: 네, 안 추워요

💬 Look at the expressions for taste and at the drinks on the menus below, and use them to role-play the dialogue with your partner.

MENU

★ 커피 ★

아이스 아메리카노

아이스 시나몬 커피

춥다

MENU

★ 전통 음료 ★

수정과

식혜

달다

MENU

★ 차 ★

홍차

인삼차

쓰다

---

1 아·아 is the abbreviated version of ice americano used in the U.S., known as iced 1 long black in Australia.

Read the following directions, then match them with the right picture.

A. 오른쪽으로 가세요.

B. 직진하세요./쭉 가세요.

C. 왼쪽으로 가세요.

D. 횡단보도를 건너세요.

1. **A. 오른쪽으로 가세요.**

2. _____

3. _____

4. _____

Haru uses a map app to move around Seoul. Where does he want to go today? How is he getting there? Look at the map application screen and answer the questions below.

1. 지금 하루가 어디에 있어요?

2. 오늘 하루가 어디에 가요?

3. 하루가 버스를 타요. 그럼 시간이 얼마나 걸려요?

4. 하루가 버스에서 내려요. 그럼 커피숍까지 얼마나 걸어가요?

5. 여러분이 길을 몰라요. 그럼 어떻게 해요? 무슨 앱을 사용해요?

📖 **After-reading activity**

Priya and Tao want to meet Haru at the coffee shop. Haru texts them instructions on how to reach him. Look at the map below and fill in the gaps in Haru's text.

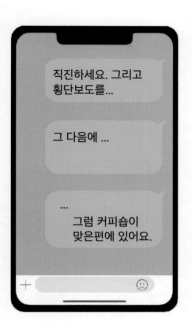

듣기 LISTENING

Pre-listening activity

Look at the table that displays traditional Korean desserts below and practice reading them with positional words like 다식이 약과 뒤에 있어요.

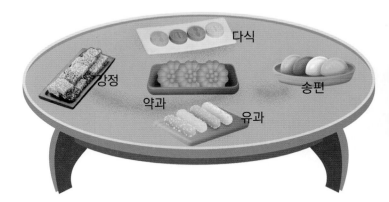

Listening activity

Haru and Sam want to visit a traditional Korean tea house (전통 찻집), so Caroline takes them to her favourite one. What types of traditional Korean desserts do they have at the tea house?

🎧 Select any dessert Caroline, Sam, and Haru choose to have from the image.

유과 강정 송편

다식 약과

🎧 Listening to the audio again, then answer the following questions and discuss them with your partner.

1. 이 찻집에서 어떤 전통 과자를 팔아요?
2. 이 찻집에서 어떤 유과가 제일 맛있어요?
3. 다식은 보통 무엇과 함께 먹어요?
4. 다식은 맛이 어때요?
5. 샘과 하루는 무엇을 주문했어요?

🎧 After-listening activity

Your partner is with Maduka. Choose one of the locations indicated on the map below, then provide them with directions to reach you there. Will they be able to find you?

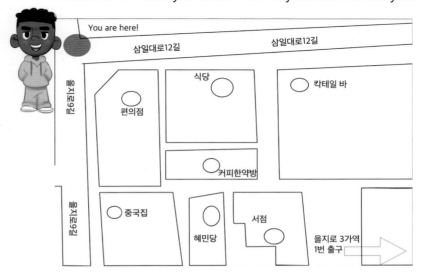

수정과 IN 아•아

A Coffee-Loving Korean:
405 Cups a Year

A Coffee-Loving Korean: 405 Cups a Year! Coffee arrived in Korea in the late 1800s during the Korean Empire, brought by diplomats and missionaries. The first known taste of coffee in Korea was by King Gojong in 1896 at the Russian legation, a scene famously shown in the drama Mr. Sunshine.

Korea's coffee culture has rapidly evolved, turning the nation into a coffee powerhouse. What began with the popularity of instant 믹스 커피 (mix coffee) —sachets of sweet and creamy instant coffee perfect for a quick caffeine fix—has grown into a vibrant café scene with endless options. From stylish, bustling cafés in Seoul to quiet neighborhood spots, coffee is now a daily ritual for many Koreans. Popular coffee terms include 아•아 (iced Americano), the favorite cooling drink, and 뜨•아 (hot Americano) for chilly days. Beyond these, specialty drinks like lattes, cold brews, and the viral Dalgona coffee have captured the hearts of many. Iconic brands such as Starbucks, Ediya, and Coffee Bean and Tea Leaf blend international and local flavors, catering to Korea's diverse tastes.

On average, Koreans consume 405 cups of coffee annually—over twice the global average of 152 cups. Coffee in Korea is more than just a drink; it's a way to unwind, connect, and embrace trends. From convenience stores to artisanal cafés, Korea's coffee culture is a testament to its adaptability and passion, making Koreans true coffee enthusiasts.

K-MEDIA CORNER

Café, tea rooms, and libraries play significant roles in Korean dramas, blending tradition, modernity, and personal growth. *Coffee Prince* features a trendy café in Seoul as the central setting, highlighting themes of love and friendship.

Sonyeon Sidae nostalgically showcases Sandara Music Tea Room, reflecting Korea's tea room culture of the 70s and 80s. *Record of Youth* uses modern cafes and the Starfield Library (별마당 도서관) to depict the dreams of young adults.

You, Whom I Met By Chance and *When My Love Blooms* highlight the warmth of traditional teas like Ssanghwa-cha (쌍화차), connecting characters to their roots and enhancing emotional depth.

 Café and tea rooms often appear in K-dramas like *Coffee Prince*. What's your favorite café scene and why?

 Traditional teas like Ssanghwa-cha appear in dramas like *You, Whom I Met By Chance*. What do you like about these cultural moments?

[이미지 출처: 네이버/유튜브]

• '얼어 죽어도 아이스 아메리카노' 의 줄임말이 얼죽아예요
→ The term is an abbreviation of the phrase 'freeze-to-death iced Americano'.

• 샘과 하루는 뭘(무엇을) 시켰어요?
→ What did Sam and Haru order?

• 이 찻집에서 코코넛 유과가 제일 맛있어요.
→ The coconut yugwa ranks as the finest snack in this tea shop.

☑ Now I know these!
Mark off what you learnt (grammar, vocabulary, usage)

• 수정과 ☑
• 가브리엘 씨는 월요일에 수영해요. 그런데 토요일 에는 수영 안 해요. ☐
• 오른쪽으로 가세요. ☐
• 광화문역에서 카페까지 버스로 16분 걸려요. ☐
• 횡단보도 맞은편에 ☐
• 다식은 좀 달아요. ☐

롤파크
(LEAGUE OF LEGENDS PARK, LOL)

Tao visits LOL Park to watch a thrilling League of Legends match, immersing himself in Korea's e-sports culture. Meanwhile the other friends remember a party they had for Sophia's birthday.

LEARNING OBJECTIVES

- Talk about individual interests and experiences.
- Describe past actions and experiences.
- Understand and use vocabulary related to recreational activities.

GRAMMAR FOCUS

- -았어요/었어요
- 못

KEY GRAMMAR AND EXPRESSIONS

1. -았어요/었어요

• MEANING AND USAGE

-았어요/었어요 is attached to the base of action verbs and descriptive verbs to indicate the past tense at an informal but polite level.

• STRUCTURE

-았어요 is attached to verb bases containing ㅏ or ㅗ, while -었어요 is attached to verb bases containing other vowels. 하다 becomes 했어요.

받다 ➡ 받 + 았어요 ➡ 받았어요
가다 ➡ 가 + 았어요 ➡ 갔어요
오다 ➡ 오 + 았어요 ➡ 왔어요

먹다 ➡ 먹 + 었어요 ➡ 먹었어요
마시다 ➡ 마시 + 었어요 ➡ 마셨어요
깨우다 ➡ 깨우 + 었어요 ➡ 깨웠어요

요리하다 ➡ 요리하 + 였어요 ➡ 요리했어요

• EXAMPLES

하루

타오 씨는 작년에 롤드컵을 봤어요?
Tao, did you see the League of Legends World Championship last year?

타오

네, 그 때 친구하고 한국에서 롤드컵을 봤어요. 너무 재미 있었어요.
Yes, I saw the League of Legends World Championship in Korea with my friend, and it was so much fun.

2. 못

• MEANING AND USAGE

못 is used in front of verbs to indicate a negative meaning when the negative action results from something beyond the subject's will. It means "cannot".

• STRUCTURE

못 is used in front of verbs; however, if the verb is a compound of noun + 해요, it is used after the noun and in front of 해요.

• EXAMPLES

어제 저녁에 요리 못 했어요. 시간이 없었어요.
→ I could not cook dinner last night. I did not have the time.

사랑 샘 씨, 점심 먹었어요?
Sam, have you had lunch?

샘 아니요. 오늘 오전에 너무 바빴어요. 그래서 아직 점심을 못 먹었어요.
No, I was swamped this morning, so I still haven't had lunch yet.

가브리엘 사랑 씨, 지난 휴일에 잘 쉬었어요?
Sarang, did you have a good rest over the holidays?

사랑 아니요. 잘 못 쉬었어요. 지난 휴일에도 편의점에서 일했어요.
No, I didn't rest well. I also worked at a convenience store during my last holiday.

Sophia and Tao are discussing the activities that Tao did yesterday.

 8-1

소피아: 타오 씨, 어제 뭐 했어요?

타오: 저는 게임을 좋아해요.
그래서 어제 e-sports 경기장에 갔어요.

소피아: 우와, 거기서 뭐 했어요?

타오: 거기서 경기를 봤어요.
그리고 선수 사인도 받았어요.

소피아: 와~ 대박!

Look at the table with details such as hobbies, locations, and activities 1 and 2. - Role-play the dialogue by replacing the information with the information in the table.

	Hobbies	Locations	Activity 1	Activity 2
1	게임	E-sports 경기장	E-sports 경기를 보다	선수 사인을 받다
2	음악	콘서트장	K-pop 콘서트를 보다	가수와 사진을 찍다
3	스포츠	야구 경기장	프로 야구 경기를 보다	치킨을 먹다
4	?	?	?	?

 READING

Pre-reading activity

What do you enjoy doing in your free time? Look at the images and determine the hobbies from the list provided.

E.g 수영해요

1. _____

2. _____

3. _____

4. _____

5. _____

6. _____

수영해요. 여행해요.
유튜브 봐요. 등산해요.
요리해요. 게임해요. 책 읽어요.

여러분 안녕하세요!
타오예요!! 잘 지냈어요?
저는 잘 지냈어요.

저는 지난 주말에 롤파크에 다녀왔어요.
왜냐하면 제 취미가 게임이에요.
특히 롤을 좋아해요. 여러분 롤 아세요?
롤은 리그 오브 레전드예요. 게임이에요.
서울에 롤파크가 있어요.
롤파크에는 e-sports 경기장이 있어요.
거기서 롤 선수들이 롤 게임을 해요.
그리고 롤파크에는 PC방도 있어요.
지난 주말에 롤 게임을 봤어요.
롤 선수들이 정말 잘했어요. 아주 재미
있었어요. 그다음에 저녁에 친구들이랑
치맥을 했어요. 프리야는 치콜을 했어요.
왜냐하면 프리야는 술을 못 마셔요.

여러분들도 롤파크에 가 보세요!!
정말 재미있어요!! 저는 다음 주에 등산
을 가요!! 북악산에 가요.
그 때 또 얘기해요!!

blog

Reading activity

This is Tao's blog, where he shares his life in Korea. Where did he go, and what did he do last weekend?

Read Tao's blog and respond to the questions below.

1. 타오 씨 취미가 뭐예요?

2. 롤파크는 어디에 있어요?

3. 타오 씨는 지난 주말에 뭐 했어요?

4. 타오 씨는 어제 친구들이랑 뭐 먹었어요? 프리야 씨는요?

5. 타오 씨는 다음 주에 어디에 가요?

After-reading activity

What did you do last weekend, and where did it happen? List your activities along with their locations in the table below to share with your friends.

E.g: Your partner: 어제 뭐 했어요?
You: 어제 노래방에서 노래를 불어요.

Your activities

	Activities	Places
1	노래를 불어요.	노래방
2		
3		
4		

Friend's activities

	Activities	Places
1		
2		
3		
4		

Pre-listening activity

Match the exclamation with the picture illustrating the situation
it might be said in.

맛있어요!

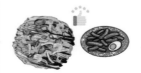

새우를 못 먹어요ㅠㅠ!

축하해요!

Listening activity

In the guesthouse living room, Haru, Sofia, and Priya talk about
Sofia's activities from the previous day. What food did Sofia eat
yesterday? What specific ingredients were in that food?

🎧 Listen to the audio file, and then select the correct statement.

1. 소피아 씨는 어제 아침에 생일 파티를 했어요.
2. 소피아 씨는 혼자 노래방에 갔어요.
3. 파전집 파전은 맛없었어요.
4. 파전집에서 떡볶이를 팔아요.

🎧 Ask and answer the following questions with your partners.

1. 파전집이 어땠어요?
2. 소피아 씨는 파전집에서 무엇을 먹었어요?
3. 누가 새우를 못 먹어요? 왜요?

Listening activity

Be a storyteller!

Imagine that you did these three activities during your recent holiday in Korea, as noted in your travel diary photo book. Begin by writing a few sentences below each photo describing those activities. Then, share with your partner what you experienced in Korea using the past tense.

MY TRAVEL DIARY: ADVANTURE PHOTO BOOK

롤파크

E.G. 롤파크에 갔어요. 롤파크는 서울에 있어요. 거기서 롤 게임을 봤어요.

한강

커피한약방

After-listening activity

Finally, use your travel photos and share them with your partner using the provided template. Remember that the past tense is necessary!

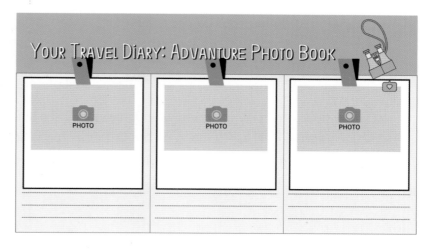

YOUR TRAVEL DIARY: ADVANTURE PHOTO BOOK

PHOTO

PHOTO

PHOTO

롤파크(LEAGUE OF LEGENDS PARK, LOL PARK)

Eating Samgyeopsal While Playing E-Games?

PC방 or internet cafés are at the heart of Korea's "Wi-Fi Republic," offering a unique blend of gaming, dining, and socializing where you can do much more than just play games— you can enjoy a full range of food, including favorites like 라면, snacks, and even sizzling 삼겹살, all without leaving your seat. The term 방 means "room" in Korean and is commonly used for various entertainment spaces like PC방 (gaming rooms) and 노래방, where people gather to relax and enjoy themselves. These rooms go beyond the activity, offering comfort, privacy, and a unique atmosphere.

A standout feature of modern PC방 is the seamless integration of "kiosk" culture, driven by rising labor costs and a demand for efficiency. From ordering food to paying for game time, self-service kiosks allow customers to customize their experience with just a few taps on a screen. Want a hot bowl of 떡볶이 or a cold soda to keep you energized during your gaming marathon? It's all just a quick order away without needing to interact with any staff. This trend towards automation extends to cafes, restaurants, and even convenience stores across Korea, making everyday transactions quicker, more convenient, and tailored to individual preferences.

This fusion of tech, gaming, and dining makes a PC방 a unique part of Korean culture. The inclusion of PC방 as "PC bang" in the Oxford English Dictionary reflects its impact, showcasing how these spaces have evolved into iconic symbols of Korea's dynamic and tech-savvy lifestyle.

K-MEDIA CORNER

PC방, or internet cafés, are key cultural hubs in Korea, appearing in dramas as places where people connect, compete, and escape. These vibrant spaces capture the social aspect of gaming, where friendships are made, rivalries emerge, and players dive into digital worlds. K-drama such as *Memories of the Alhambra* showcases augmented reality gaming, reflecting the intense atmosphere of PC Bangs.

Love Alarm highlights these spaces as social venues blending technology with daily life. *Cheese in the Trap* and *The King of Pigs* explore PC Bangs as hangouts for students and troubled youths, illustrating themes of escapism, competition, and social pressure.

 How do K-dramas like *Memories of the Alhambra* show the role of PC Bangs in Korean culture?

 What do PC Bangs in dramas like *Cheese in the Trap* and *The King of Pigs* reveal about gaming and social life in Korea?

[이미지 출처: 네이버]

- 어제 롤파크에 롤 경기 보러 갔다왔어요.
→ Yesterday, I went to the LOL park to watch the League of Legends game.

- E-SPORTS 경기도 보고 선수 사인도 받았어요.
→ I also watched an e-sports game and got a player's autograph.

- 제 취미가 게임하는 거예요.
→ Gaming is my hobby.

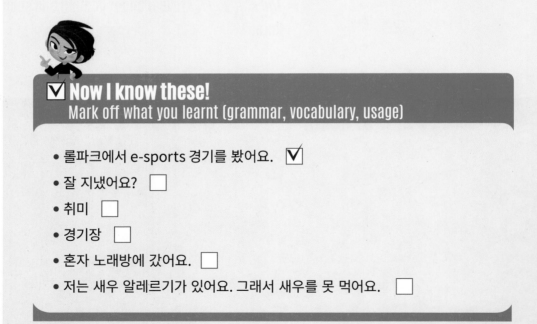

☑ Now I know these!
Mark off what you learnt (grammar, vocabulary, usage)

- 롤파크에서 e-sports 경기를 봤어요. ☑
- 잘 지냈어요? ☐
- 취미 ☐
- 경기장 ☐
- 혼자 노래방에 갔어요. ☐
- 저는 새우 알레르기가 있어요. 그래서 새우를 못 먹어요. ☐

부산행
(TRAIN TO BUSAN)

Gabriel, Sam, and Sarang plan a trip to Busan for the Busan International Film Festival. They discuss train schedules and ticketing, and experience the KTX, the Korean high speed train.

LEARNING OBJECTIVES

- Ask about train schedules and make ticket reservations.
- Make and discuss travel plans.
- Understand and use vocabulary related to booking and reservations.

GRAMMAR FOCUS

- -고 싶다
- -(으)ㄹ까요?

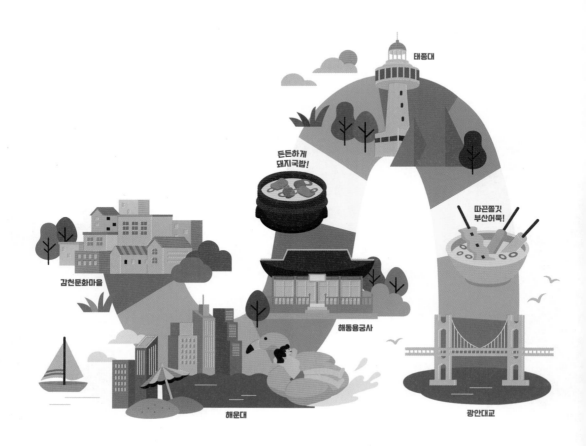

태종대

든든하게 돼지국밥!

따끈쫄깃 부산어묵!

감천문화마을

해동용궁사

해운대

광안대교

1. -고 싶다

• MEANING AND USAGE

-고 싶어요 is added to the verb base to express desire (want to "do something").

• STRUCTURE

-고 싶어요 is attached to the base of all verbs. However, when the subject, i.e. the person who wants to do something, is in the third person, then -고 싶어 해요 is used instead.

• EXAMPLES

샘

지금까지 서울만 구경을 했어. 이제는 부산에 가고 싶어.
I've only seen Seoul so far. Now I want to go to Busan.

사랑

그럼 부산에서 뭐 할 거야? 부산에서 뭐 하고 싶어?
So what are you going to do in Busan? What do you want to do in Busan?

샘

우선 자갈치 시장에 가고 싶어. 거기서 해산물을 먹고 싶어. 그리고 10월에 부산 국제화제가 있어. 거기에도 가고 싶어.
First of all, I want to go to Jagalchi (Fish) Market. I want to eat seafood there. Then there's the Busan International Film Festival in October. I want to go there, too.

샘은 부산 여행을 하고 싶어해.
→ Sam wants to go on a trip to Busan.

캐롤라인은 부산에서 부산국제영화제를 보고 싶어해.
→ Caroline wants to watch the Busan International Film Festival.

2. -(으)ㄹ까요?

• MEANING AND USAGE

The (으)ㄹ까요? is attached to the verb base. When used in the first person singular (I), it seeks the hearer's opinion. In contrast, when applied in the first person plural (we), it suggests a joint action to the hearer. This translates to English phrases like "Shall we...?" or "What about... ~ing?".

• STRUCTURE

-을까요? is attached to the base of verbs ending with a consonant, -ㄹ까요? to the base of verbs ending with a vowel. Since the meaning indicates the suggestion of doing something together, the subject is always "we."

• EXAMPLES

가브리엘 씨, 주말에 부산국제영화제에 기차 타고 갈까요? 고속 버스 타고 갈까요?

Gabriel, should we take the train to the Busan International Film Festival this weekend? Or should we take the express bus?

기차 타고 가요! 저는 차멀미를 해요.

We should take the train! I get car sick.

부산에서 뭘(무엇을) 먹을까요?

What shall we eat in Busan?

저는 밀면을 먹고 싶어요. 밀면 어때요?

I want to eat Milmyeon (wheat noodles). Do you like Milmyeon?

네! 저도 면 괜찮아요.

Yes! I like Milmyeon too.

대화 DIALOGUE

Sam is contacting a travel agency to modify his online package booking schedule.

샘: 여보세요? '헬로 투어'지요?

헬로 투어: 네, 무엇을 도와 드릴까요?

소피아: 저... 여행 날짜를 바꾸고 싶어요. 예약 번호는 ABC예요.

헬로 투어: 아, 네, 언제로 바꾸고 싶으세요?

샘: 9월 20일부터 9월 23일까지 가능할까요?

헬로 투어: 아, 죄송합니다. 그때 부산에서 부산국제화제가 있어요. 그래서 예약 변경이 어려워요

Role-play the dialogue by substituting the prompts below with colour-coded words or phrases.

여행 날짜	기차 시간	호텔
언제:	몇 시:	어느 호텔:
9월 20일부터 9월 23일까지	저녁 8시로	해운대 근처로

UNIT 9_ 부산행 (TRAIN TO BUSAN) 117

읽기 / READING

📖 Pre-reading activity

Gabriel and Sam are using the KORAIL app. What buttons do they need to click to book or purchase a ticket? Which buttons should they choose to modify or cancel their booking?

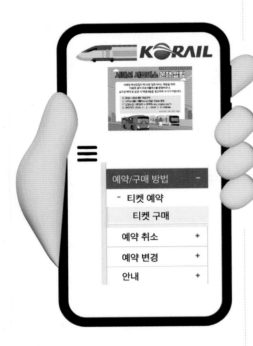

📖 Reading activity

Gabriel, Sarang, and Sam plan to travel to Busan. Sam visits the KORAIL website and notices this announcement. What steps should they take to cancel or modify their booking?

☑️ **예약 안내**
9월 20일 부터 9월 25일까지 추석 때문에 예약이 어려워요.
죄송해요.

☑️ **예약 취소/변경 방법**
여행 변경이 필요해요? 추석 이후에 여행을 하고 싶으세요?
그러면, 전화 주세요. 전화 번호는 02-2534-2333이에요.

☑️ **예약 취소/변경 안내**
• 티켓 구매 후 7일 전까지: 무료
• 수수료: 출발 1일 전: 2,000원 - 출발 3시간 전: 5% - 출발 1시간 전:10%

 헬로 투어

Read the following statements, then tick off the correct ones.

1. 사람들이 추석 때 예약을 못 해요. ☐

2. 사람들이 전화로 예약 취소/변경을 해요. ☐

3. 출발 3시간 전에 예약 취소해요.
   그럼 수수료가 없어요. ☐

4. 사람들이 출발 전에 예약 취소 못 해요. ☐

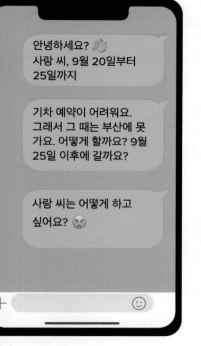

안녕하세요? 👋
사랑 씨, 9월 20일부터
25일까지

기차 예약이 어려워요.
그래서 그 때는 부산에 못
가요. 어떻게 할까요? 9월
25일 이후에 갈까요?

사랑 씨는 어떻게 하고
싶어요? 😢

After-reading activity

After reading the announcement, Sam sends a text to Sarang about their trip, saying:

What would Sarang respond? Consider her thoughts and jot down Sarang's reply to Sam's message below.

Pre-listening activity

What announcements do you usually hear while on a train in your country? What information do train attendants typically convey to passengers?

Listening activity

Sam, Gabriel and Sarang are on the train to Busan. They listen to the announcement as the train departs from Seoul and again as it approaches Busan station. What do the announcements say?

🎧 Listen to the audio and then select the correct group members.

1. 이 기차는 부산에서 출발했어요. ☐
2. 이 기차는 서울행 기차예요. ☐
3. 열차는 5분 뒤에 도착해요. ☐
4. 여러분의 가방을 꼭 가지고 내리세요. ☐

🎧 Ask and answer the following questions with your partners.

1. 이 기차는 어디서 출발했어요?
2. 언제 이 기차는 도착해요?
3. 곧 기차역에 도착해요. 그럼 사람들이 뭐 해요?

 After-listening activity

Are you planning a trip to Korea? What places are you keen on visiting, and what type of transportation do you prefer? Explore popular attractions in Korea and share your discoveries with your partner by checking out the VisitKorea website! (QR code) Present your suggestions and then propose your plan.

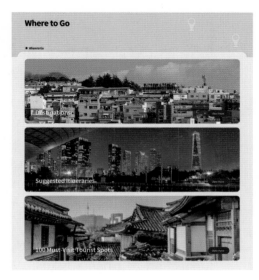

어디에 가고 싶어요?
어떻게 가요?

뭐 타고 가고 싶어요? 왜요?
거기서 뭐 하고 싶어요?

어디여기 어때요?
....에 같이 갈까요?

거기서 뭐 먹을까요?
뭐 먹고 싶어요?

'부산행'

Busan International Film Festival (BIFF)

From sleek and seductive romances like *Decision to Leave* (2021) to satirical thrillers like *Parasite* (2019), Korean films are carving out a prominent place in global cinema with a diverse and captivating spectrum of movies. Behind their rise to international prominence lies Busan, a vibrant southern port city often called the "city of film." Busan is home to the annual Busan International Film Festival (BIFF), Asia's largest film festival, which has played a pivotal role in cementing the city's reputation as a cinematic hub since its inception in 1996. Every October, cinephiles from around the world gather at the Busan Cinema Center to celebrate the best of Asian and global cinema. Busan's connection to cinema is deeply rooted in its past, with Haengjwa, one of Korea's earliest theaters, located near the port in Nampo-dong, screening films as early as the late 19th to early 20th century.

Renowned film historian Hong Young-chul, who dedicated over 45 years of his life to preserving Korean film history, often described Busan as "the birthplace of the Korean film industry." His extensive research and publications, including works like "100 Years of Busan Film" and "Modern Film History of Busan," helped lay the groundwork for the Korean Film Archives and the Busan Museum of Movies, further solidifying the city's role in shaping Korean cinema.

Korean films and dramas, fueled by platforms like Netflix, have gained global recognition for their unique narratives, emotional depth, and high production quality. Busan's rich cinematic legacy and BIFF's continued success highlight Korea's growing influence in the international film industry, making it a true powerhouse of storytelling that captivates audiences around the globe.

K-MEDIA CORNER

Busan, Korea's vibrant port city, is a popular setting in films, often highlighting its dynamic landscape and cultural significance. *Train to Busan* is a standout film, blending the thrill of a zombie apocalypse with a high-speed KTX train journey from Seoul to Busan.

It uses the train's confined space to amplify the tension between modern life and survival. *The Roundup* 2 also features Busan and the KTX, capturing a detective's chase across cities, emphasizing the role of high-speed rail in Korean life.

These films showcase Busan's cinematic appeal and how train travel reflects movement, connection, and human drama

 How do films like *Train to Busan* and *The Roundup* 2 use the setting of the KTX and the city of Busan to enhance their storytelling?

 In what ways do the portrayals of Busan in these films reflect the city's cultural and social significance in Korea?

[이미지 출처: 네이버/유튜브]

▶ Extra reading: webtoon, 라인업. *https://www.postype.com/@raadol/ series/818040*

- 예약이 꽉 찼습니다.
→ Reservation is fully booked.

- 예약이 끝났습니다.
→ The reservations have now concluded.

- 이 열차는 부산행 고속열차입니다.
→ Welcome aboard the KTX bound for Busan. (Lit. This is a high-speed train to Busan.)

- 내리실 분은 손님 여러분께서는 소지품을 가지고 내리십시오.
→ Please make sure you have all your belongings with you when leaving the train.

☑ Now I know these!
Mark off what you learnt (grammar, vocabulary, usage)

- 샘은 부산에서 부산국제영화제를 보고 싶어해.　☑
- 기차 타고 갈까요? ☐
- 예약 변경 ☐
- 취소 수수료 ☐
- 이 기차는 부산행 KTX 기차입니다. ☐

등산 맛집

Umid, Gabriel, Maka and Priya share their plan for the weekend. On the weekend, Umid and Priya join Tao on a hiking trip to the Bugaksan Mountain. Tao shares his tips for hiking essentials and the three decide to have lunch at a tofu restaurant afterward.

LEARNING OBJECTIVES

- Make, accept, or decline suggestions.
- Discuss and make suggestions about activities to carry on with other people.

GRAMMAR FOCUS

- **Descriptive verb base + -(으)ㄴ**
- **-(으)러 가다**

파전

두부김치

1. Descriptive verb base + -(으)ㄴ

• MEANING AND USAGE

-(으)ㄴ is attached to the base of descriptive verbs when the descriptive verb is used in front of a noun to describe a quality of that noun.

• STRUCTURE

-은 is attached to the base of descriptive verbs that end with a consonant, while -ㄴ is used for those ending in a vowel. However, exceptions include the words that end with 있다/없다, such as 멋있다, 멋없다, 맛있다, and 맛없다, which can take -는.

• EXAMPLES

꽃이 예뻐요. ► 예쁜 꽃
→ The flower is pretty. ► Pretty flower

저는 많은 사람들 앞에서 노래를 못 불러요.
→ I can't sing in front of many people.

북악산은 낮은 산이에요. 340m예요.
→ Bugaksan Mountain is a low mountain. It's 340 metres high.

북악산 아래에 맛있는 식당이 많아요.
→ There are many good restaurants at the bottom of Bugaksan.

가브리엘 와, 우미드 씨 그림을 잘 그려요!
Wow, Umid is good at drawing!

사랑 우미드 씨는 유명한 그래픽 디자이너예요.
Umid is a famous graphic designer.

2. -(으)러 가다

• MEANING AND USAGE

The expression -(으)러 가다, where -(으)러 is attached to the base of a verb, indicates going somewhere in order to do something. Other verbs indicating movement can be used, for example, to express the notion of coming somewhere in order to do something use -(으)러 오다.

• STRUCTURE

-으러 is attached to the base of verbs ending in a consonant, and -러 to the base of verbs ending in a vowel. Other verbs indicating movement towards a place can be used instead of 가다.

A+가 place+에 verb+(으)러 가요.
→ A goes somewhere to do something.

• EXAMPLES

가브리엘 우미드 씨, 지금 어디 가요?
Umid, where are you headed?

광화문에 아주 큰 서점이 있어요. 거기에 책 사러 가요.
There's a huge bookstore at Gwanghwa Gate. I'm going there to buy some books. **우미드**

가브리엘 서점 이름이 뭐예요?
What's the name of the bookstore?

'교보문고'예요.
It's Kyobo Bookstore. **우미드**

가브리엘 오, 저도 거기 가고 싶었어요.
I've always wanted to visit that place.

우미드 가브리엘 씨는 왜 한국에 왔어요?
Gabriel, what brings you to Korea?

저는 한국 건축[1]을 공부하러 왔어요.
I came to study Korean 1 architecture. **가브리엘**

우미드 한국 사람들이 등산복을 많이 입어요. 특히 주말에 많이 입어요.
I've seen many Koreans in hiking attire, particularly on weekends.

네, 맞아요! 한국에 산이 많아요. 주말에 등산하러 산에 많이 가요
Exactly! Korea has many mountains, and I often hike them on weekends. **가브리엘**

---

1 건축 means architecture.

대화 DIALOGUE

Umid, Gabriel, Maduka, and Priya are dining together near the guesthouse, chatting about their plans for the weekend ahead.

우미드: 내일 주말이에요. 북악산에 등산하러 갈까요?

가브리엘: 아! 미안해요. 저는 내일 부산에 가요.

우미드: 부산이요? 부산에 뭐 하러 가요?

가브리엘: 지금 부산에서 부산국제영화제를 해요. 그거 보러 가요.

우미드: 마두카 씨는요?

마두카: 죄송해요. 저는 내일 종로에 템플스테이를 하러 가요.

프리야: 우미드 씨! 저는 내일 시간 있어요! 같이 등산하러 가요!

💬 Role-play the dialogue by substituting the colour-coded words or phrases with the prompts below.

종로	템플스테이를 하다
강릉	드라마 촬영 장소를 구경하다
수원	갈비를 먹다
잠실	콘서트를 보다

READING

You are getting ready to go hiking, what would you take with you?

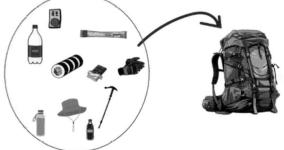

Now try to explain to your friends what you would put in your backpack.

_____   _____

_____   _____

_____   _____

Read Tao's blog. What does Tao put in his hiking backpack?

여러분!! 오늘 일요일이에요. 그리고 오늘은 날씨가 좋아요. 그래서 친구들이랑 등산하러 가요.

오늘은 북악산에 가요. 북악산은 서울에 있어요. 경복궁 근처에 있어요. 그래서 교통이 편리해요. 그리고 북악산은 높은 산이 아니에요. 그래서 저는 북악산에 등산하러 자주 가요.

<u>등산은 좋은</u> 운동이에요. 그런데 등산 중간에 피곤해요. 그래서 간식이 필요해요. 저는 보통 초콜릿하고 커피믹스를 가져가요. 그리고 가끔 배가 고파요. 그래서 저는 육포도 가방에 넣어요. 앗! 물과 수건도 꼭 필요해요! 이것들이 제 <u>등산 준비물</u>이에요. 여러분의 <u>등산 준비물은</u> 뭐예요?

저는 산 사진을 좋아해요. 그래서 오늘 산 사진도 많이 찍을 거예요.[2] 그리고 저녁에 등산 사진을 인스타그램에 올릴 거예요.

---

2 찍을 거예요 translates to 'will take a photo.' And 올릴 거예요 means 'will upload (something)'. The expression -(으)ㄹ 거예요 is attached to the action verb stem to indicate future intentions, similar to "will" in English

🎧 Ask and answer the following questions with your group members.

1. 오늘 타오 씨는 뭐 해요? ☐

2. 타오 씨는 왜 북악산 등산을 좋아해요? ☐

3. 타오 씨는 북악산에 등산하러 가요.
   무엇을 가져가요? ☐

4. 타오 씨는 오늘 사진을 많이 찍을 거예요.
   그리고 뭐 할 거예요? ☐

📖 After-reading activity

Are you interested in going somewhere this weekend? Check out the locations below, then compose a brief blog post about what you would do there and what you plan to bring with you.

북악산

DDP

DMZ

경복궁

blog

Pre-listening activity

Look at the restaurant flyer. What is the specialty of the restaurant? What is its location?

북악산
두부집
순두부
두부전
김치찌개
된장찌개
☎02) 1234-5678
북악산 입구

Listening activity

Priya and her friends just finished their hike. Where and what did they decide to eat?

🎧 Listen to the audio and answer the questions below: .

1. 프리야와 친구들은 어디에 갔어요?

2. 어디로 밥을 먹으러 가요?

3. 그 식당은 어떤 곳이에요?

4. 타오는 어떤 음식을 좋아해요?

5. 여러분은 어떤 식당을 좋아해요?
   (Describe your favourite restaurant using the expressions suggested below)

• 맛있다
• 유명하다
• 싸다
• 리뷰가 좋다
• 반찬이 많다

After-listening activity

Plan your food trip using the map below. What place do you want to visit, and what will you eat? Share your plan with your partner by telling them where you intend to eat.

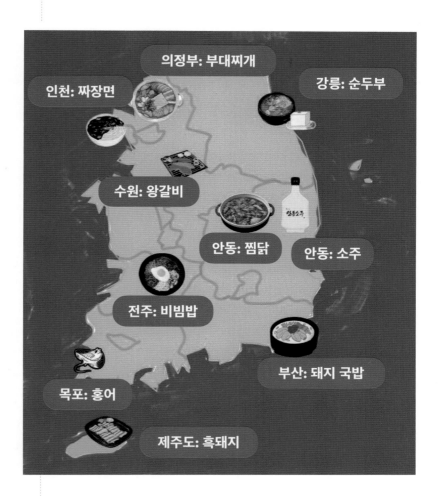

'등산 맛집'

From Ajeossi to Trendsetter:
The Rise of Deungsanbok Fashion

등산복, or hiking clothes, were once seen as the typical style of Korean 아저씨 (middle-aged men), often labeled as outdated and unfashionable. However, this perception has completely changed as 등산복 has evolved into a trendy fashion statement known as Gorpcore. This new look combines rugged outdoor style with everyday wear, making it both practical and stylish.

The Gorpcore trend gained traction when The Cut magazine first mentioned it in 2017. Not long after, luxury brands like Balenciaga and Gucci embraced the look in their collections, catapulting 등산복 into the fashion spotlight. What was once considered 아저씨 fashion has now become hip and youthful. Brands like Arc'teryx and Korean labels such as Sansan Gear are now seen on city streets, turning hiking gear into a musthave fashion trend.

The popularity of 등산복 has even reached Korean pop culture, with films like *The Himalayas*, starring Hwang Jung-min, showcasing its stylish appeal. What was once dismissed as old-fashioned has been reborn as a cool, functional choice. 등산복 has climbed from the mountains to the streets, proving that even the most practical gear can become the latest fashion sensation!

K-MEDIA CORNER

South Korea's mountainous landscape makes hiking a popular activity, often paired with dining at local 맛집, or popular restaurants near the trails. This blend of nature and food is reflected in Korean media, highlighting the connection between climbing, community, and culinary enjoyment. *The Himalayas* captures the spirit of mountaineering, showing how climbers bond over meals after challenging climbs. *Let's Eat* beautifully combines hiking and eating, as characters reward themselves with delicious food from nearby a 맛집. *Decision to Leave* uses mountain settings to reflect characters' emotions, merging stunning natural backdrops with complex storytelling.

 How do shows like *Let's Eat* and films like *The Himalayas* highlight the link between mountain climbing and eating at local restaurants in Korea?

 How do mountain settings in dramas like Decision to Leave add to the story and character experiences?

[이미지 출처: 네이버/유튜브]

실제 표현
Real expressions

- 내일 주말인데 북악산에 등산하러 갈까요?
→ The weekend starts tomorrow; shall we hike in the mountains?

- 저 식당 가서 밥 먹을까요?
→ How about dining at that restaurant?

- 저 식당이 숨은 '찐맛집'이에요.
→ That place is a hidden gem known for its steamed dishes.

☑ Now I know these!
Mark off what you learnt (grammar, vocabulary, usage)

- 내일 종로에 템플스테이를 하러 가요. ☑
- 드라마 촬영 장소 ☐
- 놓다 vs 넣다 ☐
- 교통이 편리하다 ☐
- 반찬 ☐
- 유명한 순두부찌개 맛집에 가고 싶어요. ☐

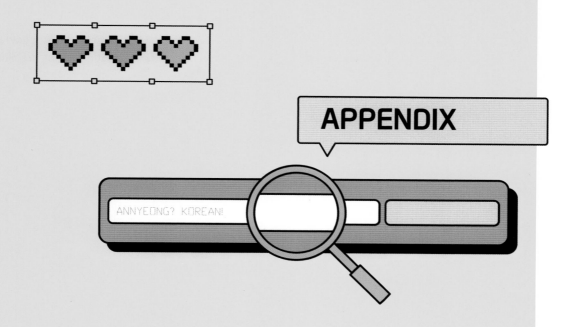

APPENDIX

ANNYEONG? KOREAN!

Appendix 01 — Numbers and Counting Words

In Korean there are two sets of numbers. Usage of the two sets depends on what is being counted. The two sets are called pure Korean numbers and Sino-Korean numbers. The pure Korean numbers are illustrated in point 1, the Sino-Korean numbers in point 2.

When using numbers to count objects or indicate quantities, the number is generally followed by a counting noun, i.e. a word indicating the category of the object counted. Counting nouns are illustrated in point 3.

1 Pure Korean Numbers

Pure Korean numbers are mainly used to tell a quantity and for counting items, age, and hours.

Pure Korean numbers:

1 하나	6 여섯	11 열하나	21 스물 하나
2 둘	7 일곱	12 열둘	22 스물둘
3 셋	8 여덟	13 열셋	…
4 넷	9 아홉	…	29 스물아홉
5 다섯	10 열	20 스물	30 서른

Tens are counted with:

10 열	40 마흔	70 일흔
20 스물	50 쉰	80 여든
30 서른	60 예순	90 아흔

When using numbers larger than 100 for counting items, it is possible to use only the Sino-Korea series of numbers (see point 2) or When counting quantities larger than one hundred use the Sino-Korean number system and use the pure Korean number system for numbers less than a hundred.

When followed by a classifier (a noun indicating a category of objects, see point 3) the following numbers are pronounced AND written differently.

1 하나 → 한 개	3 셋 → 세 개	20 스물 → 스무 개
2 둘 → 두 개	4 넷 → 네 개	

2 Sino-Korean Numbers

Sino-Korean numbers are used to tell dates, and to count things like money. They are also used to tell numbers that do not express a quantity, for example addresses, phone numbers, room numbers, or floor numbers.

✎ Sino-Korean numbers:

1 일	6 육	11 십일	21 이십일
2 이	7 칠	12 십이	22 이십이
3 삼	8 팔	13 십삼	···
4 사	9 구	···	29 이십구
5 오	10 십	20 이십	30 삼십

✎ Tens are counted with:

10 십	40 사십	70 칠십
20 이십	50 오십	80 팔십
30 삼십	60 육십	90 구십

✎ Sino-Korean numbers are used to count numbers larger than 100. Large numbers are counted as follows:

100 백	20,000 이만	10,000,000 천만
200 이백	100,000 십만	20,000,000 이천만
1,000 천	200,000 이십만	100,000,000 일억
2,000 이천	1,000,000 백만	200,000,000 이억
10,000 만	2,000,000 이백만	

✎ Telling large numbers may look hard at the beginning, but here are some examples:

65 육십오	28,000 이만 팔천
132 백삼십이	320,500 삼십이만 오백
1,782 천칠백팔십이	4,580,000 사백오십팔만

3 Counting words

In Korean, numbers can seldom be used as a stand-alone, and are generally followed by specific counting words (단위 명사), which indicate the category of the item being counted. There are numerous counting words, used for different items, people, and objects. Counting nouns can be used only with either the pure Korean numbers or the Sino-Korean numbers. Here is a guide for using numerals and their corresponding counting nouns.

The following are the most frequent counting words used with pure Korean numbers. Please note that the general counting noun is to be used only in cases the object being counted does not have a specific counting noun.

1. 개 – General

면도기 세 개만 사다 주세요! Can you please buy me just 3 razors?

2. 명/분 – People

지금 숨비소리 게스트하우스에 손님 세 명이 있어요. There are 3 guests at Sumbisori Guest house right now.

3. 권 – Books

캐롤라인 씨는 교수님이에요. 그래서 오늘 한국 역사 책 네 권을 샀어요. Caroline is a history professor, so she bought four books on Korean history today.

4. 대 – Machineries and vehicles

우미드 씨는 컴퓨터 한 대를 샀어요. Umid bought a computer.

5. 장 – Sheets, Tickets

소피아 씨는 다음 주말에 친구와 함께 케이팝 콘서트를 볼 거예요. 오늘 티켓 두 장 예약했어요. Sophia will watch a K-pop concert with her friend next week. Today she booked two tickets.

6. 마리 – Animals

사랑 씨는 고양이 두 마리한테 매일 밥을 줘요. Sarang feeds two cats at her house every day.

7. 잔 – Cups

아이스 아메리카노 한 잔 주세요. Can I have a cup of iced americano?

8. 시간 – Hours

우미드 씨는 보통 아침 일곱 시에 일어나요. Usually Umid wakes up at 7am.

9. 번 – Times/Occurrences

소피아 씨는 일주일에 세 번 한국어 수업을 들어요. Sophia takes Korean language classes three times a week.

10. 병 – Bottles

타오 씨는 편의점에서 오렌지 주스 한 병을 샀어요. Tao bought a bottle of orange juice at the convenience store.

11. 살 – Age

사랑 씨는 스물일곱 살이에요. 하루 씨는 스물두 살이에요. Sarang is 27 years old, while Haru is 22 years old.

12. 편 – Films/dramas

프리야 씨는 한국 영화를 많이 좋아해요. 주말마다 한국 영화 한 편을 봐요. Priya likes Korean films a lot. She watches one Korean film every weekend.

13. 곡 – Songs

프리야 씨는 친구들과 함께 노래방에 갔어요. 거기서 한국 노래 두 곡을 불렀어요. Priya went to the noraebang with her friends. There she sang two Korean songs.

Most frequent counting nouns used with Sino-Korean numbers:

14. 분 – Minutes

타오 씨는 저녁 일곱 시 십오 분에 한강 공원에서 친구와 만나요. Tao meets his friends at the Han river park at 7:15pm.

15. 일 Days, 월 Month*

소피아 씨는 십이 월 오 일에 한국에 갈 거예요. 비행기표를 이미 샀어요. Sophia will go to Korea on 5th December, she has already bought the flight ticket.

16. 년 Year

사랑 씨는 육 년 동안 한국에서 살았어요. Sarang has been living in Korea for six years.

17. 번 Busline

사랑 씨는 오늘 경복궁에 가요. 그래서 이백칠십삼 번 버스를 타요. Today Sarang goes to the Gyeongbok Palace. So she will take bus n. 273.

18. 원 Won (Korean currency)

올리브영에서 면도기가 한 개에 삼천 원이에요. At Olive Young they sell razors for 3,000 won each.

---

* with months and days, the following numbers are an exception:

6월 is written and pronounced as [유 월]
10월 is written and pronounced as [시 월]

Position Words

✎ **The following words are used to indicate the position and location of objects and people.**

위 up, over	옆 beside, next to
아래 below, under	사이 between, among
앞 in front	오른쪽 right side
뒤 behind	왼쪽 left side
안 inside	맞은편 in front on the opposite side
밖 outside	근처 near

✎ **Since the words above are nouns indicating a position, they are usually followed by particles indicating location and direction. They are often used with the following structure:**

▎서점이 카페 옆에 있어요. The bookstore is next to the café.

✎ **From the example above, it is possible to see that the word indicating the position (옆) is placed straight after the name indicating a location of reference (the coffee shop), and it is followed by the particle 에, which is used to indicate that something is somewhere.**

▎고양이가 식탁 위에 있어요. The cat is on the dining table.

▎하루의 가방이 책상 아래에 있어요. Haru's bag is under the desk.

▎버스 정류장이 게스트하우스 앞에 있어요. The bus stop is in front of the guesthouse.

▎프리아 씨는 가방 안에 컴퓨터를 넣었어요. Priya put the laptop inside her bag.

▎샘 씨가 친구를 야구장 밖에서 기다렸어요. Sam waited outside the baseball park for his friend.

▎카페가 중국집과 편의점 사이에 있어요. The café is between a Chinese restaurant and a convenience store.

▎숨비소리 게스트하우스는 홍대역 근처에 있어요. Sumbisori guest house is near Hongdae station.

Conjugation of Verbs

In Korean, verbs and descriptive verbs express the meaning (of the state, action, or quality), the tense, and the level of politeness. Suffixes attached to verbs and descriptive verbs do not express person, number, or gender; however, the person speaking is understandable from the context together with the level of politeness used. Understanding and using the right level of politeness is essential in Korean. Politeness in Korean has several layers, depending on either the relation among the speakers and the context. In *Annyeong? Korean!* vol. 1, we introduced a form of politeness often called "informal polite" form. It is informal because it can be used in most everyday life situations, and polite because unless when speaking with very close friends, it can be used with almost any speaker, in particular with people meeting for the first time or not very close. The informal polite form is recognisable by the ending in –요, in both the past and present tense.

Present tense

To make the present tense informal polite form, –아요 or –어요 is attached to the verb base. –아요 is attached to the base of verbs containing ㅏ or ㅗ; –어요 to the base of all other verbs. The process looks as follow:

| dictionary form | base | informal polite ending | |
| 받다 (receive) → | 받 + | 아요 | → 받아요 |

In the case of 하다 (to do), the present tense informal polite form becomes 해요.

Past tense

To make the past tense informal polite form, –았어요 or 었어요 is attached to the verb base. similarly to the present tense, –았어요 is attached to the verb of bases containing ㅏ or ㅗ, –었어요 to the base of all other verbs. 하다 at the present tense informal polite form becomes 했어요.

Summary table

Regular verbs and descriptive verbs

		Present	Past
attaching –아요	받다	받아요	받았어요
	오다	와요	왔어요
	가다	가요	갔어요
attaching –어요	먹다	먹어요	먹었어요
	배우다	배워요	배웠어요
	마시다	마셔요	마셨어요

Irregular verbs and descriptive verbs

		Present	Past
irregular in ㄷ	듣다	들어요	들었어요
irregular in —	예쁘다	예뻐요	예뻤어요
irregular in ㅂ	춥다	추워요	추웠어요
irregular in 르	모르다	몰라요	몰랐어요

Appendix 04

Word list (Korean to English, by unit)

1과

1과	개인	individual/personal
1과	게스트하우스	guest house
1과	괜찮다	okay, to be
1과	그럼	then
1과	기다리다	wait, to
1과	나라	country
1과	네	yes
1과	누구	who
1과	다음	next
1과	대학생	university student
1과	만나다	meet, to
1과	맞다 (맞아요)	correct/right, to be
1과	매니저	manager
1과	뭐	what
1과	반갑다	happy/glad, to be
1과	보여주다	show, to
1과	분	person (polite)
1과	사람	person/people
1과	소개	introduction
1과	시간	time
1과	신용카드	credit card
1과	씨	honorific suffix placed after people's name
1과	어느	which
1과	어서 오세요	Can I help you?/Welcome
1과	에어컨	air conditioning
1과	여권	passport
1과	여기	here
1과	영어	English (language)
1과	오전	morning, AM
1과	오후	afternoon, PM
1과	온돌	underfloor heating system
1과	옵션	option
1과	와이파이	wi-fi
1과	왜	why
1과	외국어	foreign language
1과	이	This
1과	이름	name
1과	일본어	Japanese (language)
1과	잠깐만	a moment, just a moment
1과	저	I (polite)
1과	정류장	bus stop
1과	주다	give, to

1과	중국어	Chinese (language)
1과	지금	now
1과	지역	region
1과	찍다	tap (a card), to
1과	체크아웃	check-out
1과	체크인	check-in
1과	터미널	terminal
1과	현금	cash
1과	화장실	toilet

2과

2과	가방	bag
2과	감사하다	thankfull, to be
2과	공항철도	airport railway
2과	그래픽 디자이너	graphic designer
2과	그런데	but, however
2과	나이지리아	Nigeria
2과	내리다	get off, to
2과	문화	culture
2과	방향	direction
2과	버스	bus
2과	선생님	teacher
2과	아니요	no
2과	우즈베키스탄	Uzbekistan
2과	유튜버	Youtuber
2과	인도네시아	Indonesia
2과	입구	entrance
2과	중국	China
2과	학생	student
2과	호텔	hotel
2과	회사원	office worker
3과	공항	airport

3과

3과	김밥	gimbap
3과	냉장고	fridge
3과	도시락	lunch box
3과	라면	ramyeon
3과	모자라다	not enough, to be
3과	바나나 우유	banana milk
3과	버거	burger
3과	봉투	plastic bag
3과	불고기	bulgogi

3과	삼각김밥	triangular gimbap
3과	샌드위치	sandwich
3과	수고하다	thank for the trouble, to
3과	심 카드	sim card
3과	아메리카노	americano
3과	아몬드	almond
3과	아이스컵	ice cup
3과	아이스크림	ice cream
3과	얼음	ice
3과	없다	be not (somewhere)/have not, to
3과	영수증	receipt
3과	원	won (Korean currency)
3과	있다	be (somewhere)/have, to
3과	적립 카드	loyalty card
3과	커피	coffee
3과	티켓	ticket
3과	편의점	convenience store
3과	프라이드 치킨	fried chicken
3과	할인	discount
3과	혹시	by any chance

4과

4과	가그린	mouth washer
4과	고맙다	thankful, to be
4과	그리고	and (connecting two actions)
4과	남자	man
4과	더	more
4과	도움	help
4과	또	again
4과	립밤	lip balm
4과	면도 크림	shaving cream
4과	면도기	razor
4과	모르다	not know, to
4과	미안하다	sorry, to be
4과	방	room
4과	선크림	sun screen
4과	세일	discount
4과	알다	know, to
4과	알리다	inform, to
4과	왁스	pommade
4과	잠시만요	wait a moment
4과	질문	question
4과	치약	toothpaste
4과	칫솔	toothbrush
4과	픽업	pick-up
4과	하고	and (connecting two nouns)
4과	향수	perfume

5과

5과	건더기	solid ingredient of a soup
5과	계란	egg
5과	공원	park
5과	굿즈 숍	merchandise shop
5과	기사님	driver
5과	기차	train
5과	내일	tomorrow
5과	넣다	put in, to
5과	누르다	press, to
5과	담요	blanket
5과	대다	tap, to
5과	돗자리	mat
5과	드시다	eat, to (polite)
5과	말하다	speak/say, to
5과	맵다	spicy, to be
5과	면	noodles
5과	몇	how many
5과	물	water
5과	받다	receive, to
5과	버튼	button
5과	병	bottle
5과	분	minute
5과	스프	soup
5과	어제	yesterday
5과	얼마	how much
5과	오늘	today
5과	저녁	evening
5과	젓가락	chopsticks
5과	참깨	sesame
5과	카드 (교통)	card (transportation)
5과	필요하다	necessary, to be
5과	후	after

6과

6과	가이드 투어	guided tour
6과	기차역	train station
6과	공부	study
6과	관람료	admission fee (to an exhibition, cinema etc)
6과	광장	square
6과	교통	transportation/traffic
6과	구경하다	sightseeing, to
6과	국립	national
6과	금요일	Friday
6과	기념관	memorial hall
6과	기념품	souvenir
6과	드라마	drama
6과	듣다	hear, to
6과	많이	a lot of, many
6과	매주	every week

6과	먹다	eat, to	
6과	목요일	Thursday	
6과	무료	free (of charge)	
6과	바쁘다	busy, to be	
6과	박물관	museum	
6과	배우다	learn, to	
6과	보다	see/watch, to	
6과	보통	usually	
6과	사다	buy, to	
6과	사진	photograph	
6과	서비스	service	
6과	선물	gift, present	
6과	설명하다	explain, to	
6과	수어	sign language	
6과	수요일	Wednesday	
6과	숙박하다	stay/lodge, to	
6과	엘리베이터	elevator	
6과	역사	history	
6과	열다	open, to	
6과	요즘	recently	
6과	월요일	Monday	
6과	이야기	story	
6과	일요일	Sunday	
6과	자주	often	
6과	지하철역	subway station	
6과	장소	place	
6과	전시회	exhibition	
6과	전쟁	war	
6과	정문	main entrance	
6과	제목	title	
6과	좋다	good, to be	
6과	주말	weekend	
6과	주중	weekdays	
6과	찍다	take (a photograph), to	
6과	참	exclamation	
6과	추천하다	suggest, to	
6과	층	floor, level	
6과	캠핑	camping	
6과	토요일	Saturday	
6과	평화	peace	
6과	하다	do, to	
6과	화요일	Tuesday	
6과	휠체어	wheelchair	
6과	휴관	closure day (of a museum)	

7과

7과	갑자기	suddenly
7과	건너다	cross, to
7과	걷다	walk, to
7과	걸리다	take (time), to
7과	게임	game (video games)

7과	고양이	cat
7과	꼭 for	sure
7과	놓다	put, to
7과	달다	sweet, to be
7과	뜻	meaning
7과	마시다	drink, to
7과	문	door
7과	병원	hospital
7과	비	rain
7과	수정과	cold cinnamon punch
7과	시나몬	cinnamon
7과	식혜	sweet rice drink
7과	신다	wear (shoes), to
7과	신발	shoes
7과	쓰다	bitter, to be
7과	아아 (아이스 아메리카노)	ice americano
7과	영화	film
7과	오른쪽	right side
7과	왼쪽	left side
7과	우산	umbrella
7과	음료	beverage
7과	인삼차	ginseng tea
7과	좋아하다	like, to
7과	직진하다	go straight, to
7과	진짜	really
7과	차	tea
7과	춥다	cold, to be
7과	친구	friend
7과	홍차	black tea
7과	횡단보도	pedestrian crossing

8과

8과	경기	match, game
8과	경기장	stadium
8과	너무	too much
8과	다니다	go (regularly)/attend, to
8과	대박	awesome
8과	등산하다	go hiking, to
8과	롤	League of Legends (game)
8과	사인	autograph
8과	새우	shrimp
8과	선수	player/athlete
8과	수영하다	swim, to
8과	쉬다	rest, to
8과	아직	yet (not yet)
8과	아침	morning
8과	야구	baseball
8과	왜냐하면	because
8과	요리하다	cook, to
8과	음악	music

8과	읽다	read, to
8과	작년	last year
8과	재미있다	fun/interesting, to be
8과	점심	lunch
8과	지난	past, last
8과	지내다	spend/pass, to
8과	책	book
8과	축하하다	congratulate, to
8과	취미	hobby
8과	콘서트장	concert stadium/place
8과	특히	in particular
8과	파전	green onion pancake
8과	팔다	sell, to
8과	혼자	alone
8과	휴일	holiday

9과

9과	가능하다	possible, to be
9과	가지다	carry, to
9과	같이	together
9과	고속열차	high speed train
9과	곧	soon
9과	구매하다	purchase, to
9과	국제영화제	international film festival
9과	까지	to
9과	끝나다	finished, to be
9과	날짜	day, date
9과	도와주다	help, to
9과	도착하다	arrive, to
9과	멀미	sickness (travel, car, sea etc…)
9과	미리	in advance
9과	밀면	wheat noodles
9과	바꾸다	change, to
9과	번호	number
9과	변경	change
9과	부터	from
9과	소지품	personal belonging
9과	수수료	commission, charge
9과	시장	market
9과	어렵다	difficult, to be
9과	여보세요	hello (over the phone)
9과	여행	travel
9과	열차	train
9과	예약	booking
9과	이용하다	use, to
9과	이후	afterward
9과	죄송하다	sorry, to be
9과	차다	full, to be
9과	추석	Autumn moon festivities

9과	출발	departure
9과	취소	cancellation
9과	타다	take a transportation, to

10과

10과	가끔	sometimes
10과	간식	snack
10과	갈비	ribs
10과	건축	architecture
10과	고프다	hungry, to be
10과	그리다	draw, to
10과	그림	drawing
10과	김치찌개	kimchi stew
10과	꽃	flower
10과	날씨	weather
10과	낮다	low, to be
10과	높다	high, to be
10과	된장찌개	soybean paste stew
10과	두부전	fried tofu
10과	등산 코스	hiking path
10과	디자이너	designer
10과	리뷰	review
10과	맛있다	yummy, to be
10과	맛집	a must-go restaurant
10과	반찬	side dish
10과	산	mountain
10과	서점	bookstore
10과	수건	towel
10과	순두부	spicy tofu soup
10과	식당	restaurant
10과	싸다	cheap, to be
10과	엄청	very much, terribly
10과	예쁘다	beautiful/pretty, to be
10과	운동	sport
10과	유명하다	famous, to be
10과	육포	beef jerky
10과	음식	food
10과	준비물	items needed, items to prepare
10과	중간	middle
10과	초콜릿	chocolate
10과	촬영	filming (photo, drama, film, video)
10과	커피믹스	instant coffee
10과	템플스테이	temple stay
10과	피곤하다	tired, to be

Word list (Korean to English)

ㄱ, ㄲ

4과	가그린	mouth washer
10과	가끔	sometimes
9과	가능하다	possible, to be
2과	가방	bag
6과	가이드 투어	guided tour
9과	가지다	carry, to
10과	간식	snack
10과	갈비	ribs
2과	감사하다	thankfull, to be
7과	갑자기	suddenly
9과	같이	together
1과	개인	individual/personal
7과	건너다	cross, to
5과	건더기	solid ingredient of a soup
10과	건축	architecture
7과	걷다	walk, to
7과	걸리다	take (time), to
1과	게스트하우스	guest house
7과	게임	game (video games)
8과	경기	match, game
8과	경기장	stadium
5과	계란	egg
4과	고맙다	thankful, to be
9과	고속열차	high speed train
7과	고양이	cat
10과	고프다	hungry, to be
9과	곧	soon
6과	공부	study
5과	공원	park
3과	공항	airport
2과	공항철도	airport railway
6과	관람료	admission fee (to an exhibition, cinema etc)
6과	광장	square
1과	괜찮다	okay, to be
6과	교통	transportation/traffic
6과	구경하다	sightseeing, to
9과	구매하다	purchase, to
6과	국립	national
9과	국제영화제	international film festival
5과	굿즈 숍	merchandise shop
2과	그래픽 디자이너	graphic designer
2과	그런데	but, however

1과	그럼	then
4과	그리고	and (connecting two actions)
10과	그리다	draw, to
10과	그림	drawing
6과	금요일	Friday
6과	기념관	memorial hall
6과	기념품	souvenir
1과	기다리다	wait, to
5과	기사님	driver
5과	기차	train
6과	기차역	train station
3과	김밥	gimbap
10과	김치찌개	kimchi stew
9과	까지	to
7과	꼭	for sure
10과	꽃	flower
9과	끝나다	finished, to be

ㄴ

1과	나라	country
2과	나이지리아	Nigeria
10과	날씨	weather
9과	날짜	day, date
4과	남자	man
10과	낮다	low, to be
2과	내리다	get off, to
5과	내일	tomorrow
3과	냉장고	fridge
8과	너무	too much
5과	넣다	put in, to
1과	네	yes
10과	높다	high, to be
7과	놓다	put, to
1과	누구	who
5과	누르다	press, to

ㄷ, ㄸ

8과	다니다	go (regularly)/attend, to
1과	다음	next
7과	달다	sweet, to be
5과	담요	blanket
5과	대다	tap, to

8과	대박	awesome
1과	대학생	university student
4과	더	more
3과	도시락	lunch box
9과	도와주다	help, to
4과	도움	help
9과	도착하다	arrive, to
5과	돗자리	mat
10과	된장찌개	soybean paste stew
10과	두부전	fried tofu
6과	드라마	drama
5과	드시다	eat, to (polite)
6과	듣다	hear, to
10과	등산 코스	hiking path
8과	등산하다	go hiking, to
10과	디자이너	designer
4과	또	again
7과	뜻	meaning

ㄹ		
3과	라면	ramyeon
8과	롤	League of Legends (game)
10과	리뷰	review
4과	립밤	lip balm

ㅁ		
7과	마시다	drink, to
1과	만나다	meet, to
6과	많이	a lot of, many
5과	말하다	speak/say, to
10과	맛있다	yummy, to be
10과	맛집	a must-go restaurant
1과	맞다 (맞아요)	correct/right, to be
1과	매니저	manager
6과	매주	every week
5과	맵다	spicy, to be
6과	먹다	eat, to
9과	멀미	sickness (travel, car, sea etc…)
5과	면	noodles
4과	면도 크림	shaving cream
4과	면도기	razor
5과	몇	how many
4과	모르다	not know, to
3과	모자라다	not enough, to be
6과	목요일	Thursday
6과	무료	free (of charge)
7과	문	door
2과	문화	culture

5과	물	water
1과	뭐	what
9과	미리	in advance
4과	미안하다	sorry, to be
9과	밀면	wheat noodles

ㅂ		
9과	바꾸다	change, to
3과	바나나 우유	banana milk
6과	바쁘다	busy, to be
6과	박물관	museum
1과	반갑다	happy/glad, to be
10과	반찬	side dish
5과	받다	receive, to
4과	방	room
2과	방향	direction
6과	배우다	learn, to
3과	버거	burger
2과	버스	bus
5과	버튼	button
9과	번호	number
9과	변경	change
5과	병	bottle
7과	병원	hospital
6과	보다	see/watch, to
1과	보여주다	show, to
6과	보통	usually
3과	봉투	plastic bag
9과	부터	from
1과	분	person (polite)
5과	분	minute
3과	불고기	bulgogi
7과	비	rain

ㅅ, ㅆ		
6과	사다	buy, to
1과	사람	person/people
8과	사인	autograph
6과	사진	photograph
10과	산	mountain
3과	삼각김밥	triangular gimbap
8과	새우	shrimp
3과	샌드위치	sandwich
6과	서비스	service
10과	서점	bookstore
6과	선물	gift, present
2과	선생님	teacher
8과	선수	player/athlete

4과	선크림	sun screen
6과	설명하다	explain, to
4과	세일	discount
1과	소개	introduction
9과	소지품	personal belonging
10과	수건	towel
3과	수고하다	thank for the trouble, to
9과	수수료	commission, charge
6과	수어	sign language
8과	수영하다	swim, to
6과	수요일	Wednesday
7과	수정과	cold cinnamon punch
6과	숙박하다	stay/lodge, to
10과	순두부	spicy tofu soup
8과	쉬다	rest, to
5과	스프	soup
1과	시간	time
7과	시나몬	cinnamon
9과	시장	market
10과	식당	restaurant
7과	식혜	sweet rice drink
7과	신다	wear (shoes), to
7과	신발	shoes
1과	신용카드	credit card
3과	심 카드	sim card
10과	싸다	bitter, to be
1과	씨	honorific suffix placed after people's name

ㅇ

2과	아니요	no
3과	아메리카노	americano
3과	아몬드	almond
7과	아아 (아이스 아메리카노)	ice americano
3과	아이스컵	ice cup
3과	아이스크림	ice cream
8과	아직	yet (not yet)
8과	아침	morning
4과	알다	know, to
4과	알리다	inform, to
8과	야구	baseball
1과	어느	which
9과	어렵다	difficult, to be
1과	어서 오세요	Can I help you?/Welcome
5과	어제	yesterday
5과	얼마	how much
3과	얼음	ice
10과	엄청	very much, terribly
3과	없다	be not (somewhere)/have not, to
1과	에어컨	air conditioning

6과	엘리베이터	elevator
1과	여권	passport
1과	여기	here
9과	여보세요	hello (over the phone)
9과	여행	travel
6과	역사	history
6과	열다	open, to
9과	열차	train
3과	영수증	receipt
1과	영어	English (language)
7과	영화	film
10과	예쁘다	beautiful/pretty, to be
9과	예약	booking
5과	오늘	today
7과	오른쪽	right side
1과	오전	morning, AM
1과	오후	afternoon, PM
1과	온돌	underfloor heating system
1과	옵션	option
1과	와이파이	wi-fi
4과	왁스	pommade
1과	왜	why
8과	왜냐하면	because
1과	외국어	foreign language
7과	왼쪽	left side
8과	요리하다	cook, to
6과	요즘	recently
7과	우산	umbrella
2과	우즈베키스탄	Uzbekistan
10과	운동	sport
3과	원	won (Korean currency)
6과	월요일	Monday
10과	유명하다	famous, to be
2과	유튜버	Youtuber
10과	육포	beef jerky
7과	음료	beverage
10과	음식	food
8과	음악	music
1과	이	This
1과	이름	name
6과	이야기	story
9과	이용하다	use, to
9과	이후	afterward
2과	인도네시아	Indonesia
7과	인삼차	ginseng tea
1과	일본어	Japanese (language)
6과	일요일	Sunday
8과	읽다	read, to
2과	입구	entrance
3과	있다	be (somewhere)/have, to

ㅈ, ㅊ

6과	자주	often
6과	지하철역	subway station
8과	작년	last year
1과	잠깐만	a moment, just a moment
4과	잠시만요	wait a moment
6과	장소	place
8과	재미있다	fun/interesting, to be
1과	저	I (polite)
5과	저녁	evening
3과	적립카드	loyalty card
6과	전시회	exhibition
6과	전쟁	war
8과	점심	lunch
5과	젓가락	chopsticks
1과	정류장	bus stop
6과	정문	main entrance
6과	제목	title
6과	좋다	good, to
9과	죄송하다	sorry, to be
1과	주다	give, to
6과	주말	weekend
6과	주중	weekdays
10과	준비물	items needed, items to prepare
10과	중간	middle
2과	중국	China
1과	중국어	Chinese (language)
1과	지금	now
8과	지난	past, last
8과	지내다	spend/pass, to
1과	지역	region
7과	직진하다	go straight, to
7과	진짜	really
4과	질문	question
1과	찍다	tap (a card), to
6과	찍다	take (a photograph), to
7과	차	tea
9과	차다	full, to be
6과	참	exclamation
5과	참깨	sesame
8과	책	book
1과	체크아웃	check-out
1과	체크인	check-in
10과	초콜릿	chocolate
10과	촬영	filming (photo, drama, film, video)
9과	추석	Autumn moon festivities
6과	추천하다	suggest, to
8과	축하하다	congratulate, to
9과	출발	departure

7과	춥다	cold, to be
8과	취미	hobby
9과	취소	cancellation
6과	층	floor, level
4과	치약	toothpaste
7과	친구	friend
4과	칫솔	toothbrush

ㅋ, ㅌ, ㅍ, ㅎ

5과	카드 (교통)	card (transportation)
6과	캠핑	camping
3과	커피	coffee
10과	커피믹스	instant coffee
8과	콘서트장	concert stadium/place
9과	타다	take a transportation, to
1과	터미널	terminal
10과	템플스테이	temple stay
6과	토요일	Saturday
8과	특히	in particular
3과	티켓	ticket
8과	파전	green onion pancake
8과	팔다	sell, to
3과	편의점	convenience store
6과	평화	peace
3과	프라이드 치킨	fried chicken
10과	피곤하다	tired, to be
4과	픽업	pick-up
5과	필요하다	necessary, to be
4과	하고	and (connecting two nouns)
6과	하다	do, to
2과	학생	student
3과	할인	discount
4과	향수	perfume
1과	현금	cash
2과	호텔	hotel
3과	혹시	by any chance
8과	혼자	alone
7과	홍차	black tea
6과	화요일	Tuesday
1과	화장실	toilet
2과	회사원	office worker
7과	횡단보도	pedestrian crossing
5과	후	after
6과	휠체어	wheelchair
6과	휴관	closure day (of a museum)
8과	휴일	holiday

Word list (English to Korean)

A

6과	a lot of, many	많이
1과	a moment, just a moment	잠깐만
10과	a must-go restaurant	맛집
6과	admission fee (to an exhibition, cinema etc)	관람료
5과	after	후
1과	afternoon, PM	오후
9과	afterward	이후
4과	again	또
1과	air conditioning	에어컨
3과	airport	공항
2과	airport railway	공항철도
3과	almond	아몬드
8과	alone	혼자
3과	americano	아메리카노
4과	and (connecting two actions)	그리고
4과	and (connecting two nouns)	하고
10과	architecture	건축
9과	arrive, to	도착하다
8과	autograph	사인
9과	Autumn moon festivities	추석
8과	awesome	대박

B

2과	bag	가방
3과	banana milk	바나나 우유
8과	baseball	야구
3과	be not (somewhere)/have not, to	없다
10과	beautiful/pretty, to be	예쁘다
8과	because	왜냐하면
10과	beef jerky	육포
3과	be, to	있다
7과	beverage	음료
7과	bitter, to be	쓰다
7과	black tea	홍차
5과	blanket	담요
8과	book	책
9과	booking	예약
10과	bookstore	서점
5과	bottle	병
3과	bulgogi	불고기
3과	burger	버거
2과	bus	버스
1과	bus stop	정류장

6과	busy, to be	바쁘다
2과	but, however	그런데
5과	button	버튼
6과	buy, to	사다
3과	by any chance	혹시

C

6과	camping	캠핑
1과	Can I help you?	어서 오세요
9과	cancellation	취소
5과	card (transportation)	카드 (교통)
9과	carry, to	가지다
1과	cash	현금
7과	cat	고양이
9과	change	변경
9과	change, to	바꾸다
10과	cheap, to be	싸다
1과	check-in	체크인
1과	check-out	체크아웃
2과	China	중국
1과	Chinese (language)	중국어
10과	chocolate	초콜릿
5과	chopsticks	젓가락
7과	cinnamon	시나몬
6과	closure day (of a museum)	휴관
3과	coffee	커피
7과	cold cinnamon punch	수정과
7과	cold, to be	춥다
9과	commission, charge	수수료
8과	concert stadium/place	콘서트장
8과	congratulate, to	축하하다
3과	convenience store	편의점
8과	cook, to	요리하다
1과	correct/right, to be	맞다 (맞아요)
1과	country	나라
1과	credit card	신용카드
7과	cross, to	건너다
2과	culture	문화

D

9과	day, date	날짜
9과	departure	출발
10과	designer	디자이너
9과	difficult, to be	어렵다
2과	direction	방향

4과	discount	세일
3과	discount	할인
6과	do, to	하다
7과	door	문
6과	drama	드라마
10과	draw, to	그리다
10과	drawing	그림
7과	drink, to	마시다
5과	driver	기사님

E

6과	eat, to	먹다
5과	eat, to (polite)	드시다
5과	egg	계란
6과	elevator	엘리베이터
1과	English (language)	영어
2과	entrance	입구
8과	last year	작년
5과	evening	저녁
6과	every week	매주
6과	exclamation	참
6과	exhibition	전시회
6과	explain, to	설명하다

F

10과	famous, to be	유명하다
7과	film	영화
10과	filming (photo, drama, film, video)	촬영
9과	finished, to be	끝나다
6과	floor, level	층
10과	flower	꽃
10과	food	음식
7과	for sure	꼭
1과	foreign language	외국어
6과	free (of charge)	무료
6과	Friday	금요일
3과	fridge	냉장고
3과	fried chicken	프라이드 치킨
10과	fried tofu	두부전
7과	friend	친구
9과	from	부터
9과	full, to be	차다
8과	fun/interesting, to be	재미있다

G

7과	game (video games)	게임
2과	get off, to	내리다
6과	gift, present	선물

3과	gimbap	김밥
7과	ginseng tea	인삼차
1과	give, to	주다
8과	go (regularly)/attend, to	다니다
8과	go hiking, to	등산하다
7과	go straight, to	직진하다
6과	good, to be	좋다
2과	graphic designer	그래픽 디자이너
8과	green onion pancake	파전
1과	guest house	게스트하우스
6과	guided tour	가이드 투어

H

1과	happy/glad, to be	반갑다
6과	hear, to	듣다
9과	hello (over the phone)	여보세요
4과	help	도움
9과	help, to	도와주다
1과	here	여기
9과	high speed train	고속열차
10과	high, to be	높다
10과	hiking path	등산 코스
6과	history	역사
8과	hobby	취미
8과	holiday	휴일
1과	honorific suffix placed after people's name	씨
7과	hospital	병원
2과	hotel	호텔
5과	how many	몇
5과	how much	얼마
10과	hungry, to be	고프다

I, J, K, L

1과	I (polite)	저
3과	ice	얼음
7과	ice americano	아아(아이스 아메리카노)
3과	ice cream	아이스크림
3과	ice cup	아이스컵
9과	in advance	미리
8과	in particular	특히
1과	individual/personal	개인
2과	Indonesia	인도네시아
4과	inform, to	알리다
10과	instant coffee	커피믹스
9과	international film festival	국제영화제
1과	introduction	소개
10과	items needed, items to prepare	준비물
1과	Japanese (language)	일본어
10과	kimchi stew	김치찌개
4과	know, to	알다

8과	League of Legends (game)	롤
6과	learn, to	배우다
7과	left side	왼쪽
7과	like, to	좋아하다
4과	lip balm	립밤
10과	low, to be	낮다
3과	loyalty card	적립카드
8과	lunch	점심
3과	lunch box	도시락

M, N

6과	main entrance	정문
4과	man	남자
1과	manager	매니저
9과	market	시장
5과	mat	돗자리
8과	match, game	경기
7과	meaning	뜻
1과	meet, to	만나다
6과	memorial hall	기념관
5과	merchandise shop	굿즈 숍
10과	middle	중간
5과	minute	분
6과	Monday	월요일
4과	more	더
8과	morning	아침
1과	morning, AM	오전
10과	mountain	산
4과	mouth washer	가그린
6과	museum	박물관
8과	music	음악
1과	name	이름
6과	national	국립
5과	necessary, to be	필요하다
1과	next	다음
2과	Nigeria	나이지리아
2과	no	아니요
5과	noodles	면
3과	not enough, to be	모자라다
4과	not know, to	모르다
1과	now	지금
9과	number	번호

O, P, Q, R

2과	office worker	회사원
6과	often	자주
1과	okay, to be	괜찮다
6과	open, to	열다
1과	option	옵션
5과	park	공원
1과	passport	여권
8과	past, last	지난
6과	peace	평화
7과	pedestrian crossing	횡단보도
4과	perfume	향수
1과	person (polite)	분
1과	person/people	사람
9과	personal belonging	소지품
6과	photograph	사진
4과	pick-up	픽업
6과	place	장소
3과	plastic bag	봉투
8과	player/athlete	선수
4과	pommade	왁스
9과	possible, to be	가능하다
5과	press, to	누르다
9과	purchase, to	구매하다
5과	put in, to	넣다
7과	put, to	놓다
4과	question	질문
7과	rain	비
3과	ramyeon	라면
4과	razor	면도기
8과	read, to	읽다
7과	really	진짜
3과	receipt	영수증
5과	receive, to	받다
6과	recently	요즘
1과	region	지역
8과	rest, to	쉬다
10과	restaurant	식당
10과	review	리뷰
10과	ribs	갈비
7과	right side	오른쪽
4과	room	방

S

3과	sandwich	샌드위치
6과	Saturday	토요일
6과	see/watch, to	보다
8과	sell, to	팔다
6과	service	서비스
5과	sesame	참깨
4과	shaving cream	면도 크림
7과	shoes	신발
1과	show, to	보여주다
8과	shrimp	새우
9과	sickness (travel, car, sea etc…)	멀미
10과	side dish	반찬

6과	sightseeing, to	구경하다
6과	sign language	수어
3과	sim card	심 카드
10과	snack	간식
5과	solid ingredient of a soup	건더기
10과	sometimes	가끔
9과	soon	곧
4과	sorry, to be	미안하다
9과	sorry, to be	죄송하다
5과	soup	스프
6과	souvenir	기념품
10과	soybean paste stew	된장찌개
5과	speak/say, to	말하다
8과	spend/pass, to	지내다
10과	spicy tofu soup	순두부
5과	spicy, to be	맵다
10과	sport	운동
6과	square	광장
8과	stadium	경기장
6과	stay/lodge, to	숙박하다
6과	story	이야기
2과	student	학생
6과	study	공부
6과	subway station	지하철역
7과	suddenly	갑자기
6과	suggest, to	추천하다
4과	sun screen	선크림
6과	Sunday	일요일
7과	sweet rice drink	식혜
7과	sweet, to be	달다
8과	swim, to	수영하다

T

6과	take (a photograph), to	찍다
7과	take (time), to	걸리다
9과	take a transportation, to	타다
5과	tap, to	대다
1과	tap (a card), to	찍다
7과	tea	차
2과	teacher	선생님
10과	temple stay	템플스테이
1과	terminal	터미널
3과	thank for the trouble, to	수고하다
4과	thankful, to be	고맙다
2과	thankfull, to be	감사하다
1과	then	그럼
1과	This	이
6과	Thursday	목요일
3과	ticket	티켓
1과	time	시간
10과	tired, to be	피곤하다

6과	title	제목
9과	to	까지
5과	today	오늘
9과	together	같이
1과	toilet	화장실
5과	tomorrow	내일
8과	too much	너무
4과	thbrush	칫솔
4과	toothpaste	치약
10과	towel	수건
5과	train	기차
9과	train	열차
6과	train station	기차역
6과	transportation/traffic	교통
9과	travel	여행
3과	triangular gimbap	삼각김밥
6과	Tuesday	화요일

U, V, W, Y

7과	umbrella	우산
1과	underfloor heating system	온돌
1과	university student	대학생
9과	use, to	이용하다
6과	usually	보통
2과	Uzbekistan	우즈베키스탄
10과	very much, terribly	엄청
4과	wait a moment	잠시만요
1과	wait, to	기다리다
7과	walk, to	걷다
6과	war	전쟁
5과	water	물
7과	wear (shoes), to	신다
10과	weather	날씨
6과	Wednesday	수요일
6과	weekdays	주중
6과	weekend	주말
1과	Welcome	어서 오세요
1과	what	뭐
9과	wheat noodles	밀면
6과	wheel chair	휠체어
1과	which	어느
1과	who	누구
1과	why	왜
1과	wi-fi	와이파이
3과	won (Korean currency)	원
1과	yes	네
5과	yesterday	어제
8과	yet (not yet)	아직
2과	Youtuber	유튜버
10과	yummy, to be	맛있다

Answer to exercises

1과

Pre-reading activity	화장실 – 1; 와이파이 – 4; 온돌 – 2; 에어컨 – 3
Reading	체크인 시간– 1; 외국어– 1; 옵션 – 3
After-reading activity	와이파이; 체크아웃; 에어컨; 중국어; 화장실; 온돌; 안녕하세요?
Pre-listening activity	현금 – 3; 여기 찍으세요 – 1; 신용 카드 – 2
Listening activity	안녕하세요?; 신용 카드; 현금; 여기에 찍으세요

2과

Pre-reading activity	우버; 택시; 기차; 버스
Reading	신촌 방향
After-reading activity	더플라자 호텔 – 시청 방향; 머큐어 호텔 – 신촌 방향; 웨스틴 조선(서울) 호텔 – 시청 방향; 더리버사이드 호텔 – 강남 방향
Pre-listening activity	1. 이 아니에요; 2. 여기; 3. 다음
Listening activity	뉴서울 호텔
Activity	**Word search puzzle!** 관 러 푸 언 경 원 예 듀 술 머 연 로 화 팜 서 회 듀 경 농 에 듀 농 얼 머 사 풀 찰 듀 학 서 리 이 가 원 디 관 디 재 풀 게 술 어 이 자 부 경 안 로 예 원 영 이 너 게 이 프 서 영 화 배 우 회 관 스 마 트 팜 농 부 찰 듀 회 어 듀 너 농 경 다 자 아 나

3과

Reading	불고기 버거; 아메리카노; 소프트 아이스크림; 프라이드 치킨
Pre-listening activity	봉투 – 3; 100원 – 2; 5,000원 – 1
Listening activity	1; 3

Pre-reading activity	1. 냉장고; 2. 세탁기; 3. 화장실; 4. 치약/칫솔; 5. 와이파이
Reading	1. 마두카 씨는 나이지리아 사람이에요; 2. 마두카 씨는 3월 1일에 한국에 가요; 3. 방이 있어요? 와이파이와 에어컨이 있어요? 공항 픽업이 있어요?
After-reading activity	1; 2
Pre-listening activity	1. 한, 더; 2. 네
Listening activity	면도기 3개 + 립밤 3개

Pre-reading activity	1. 물; 2. 면; 3. 젓가락; 4. 건더기; 5. 계란; 6. 스프
Reading	Between step 4 and step 5
After-reading activity	A – F – B – D – C – E
Pre-listening activity	1. 기다리세요, 카드; 2. 한 장
Listening activity	기사님, 2명이에요 〉 잠깐만요 기다리세요 〉 지금 카드를 대세요

Pre-reading activity	1. 무료; 2. 휴관; 3. 주중; 4. 주말
Reading	2, 5
Pre-listening activity	전시관 – 선생님: "이쪽에 있어요"; 광장 – 정문 뒤에 있어요; 주차장 – "식당 근처에 있어요"; 식당 – 선생님: "저쪽에 있어요"
Listening activity	A) 정문, 광장, 어린이 박물관, 주차장, 카페, 화장실; B) 1, 3

Pre-reading activity	2 – D; 3 – B; 4 – C
Reading	1. 지금 하루는 교보문고 광화문점에 있어요; 2. 오늘 하루는 커피한약방에 가요; 3. 7분; 4. 5분 걸어요.
After-reading activity	직진하세요. 그리고 횡단보도를 건너세요. 그 다음 왼쪽으로 가세요. 그리고 직진하세요. 그 다음에 오른쪽, 왼쪽으로 가세요. 카페가 왼쪽에 있어요. 3분 쯤 걸려요.
Listening activity	A) 약과, 강정, 유과, 다식; B) 1. 약과, 강정, 유과, 다식을 팔아요; 2. 코코넛 유과가 제일 맛있어요; 3. 차하고 같이 마셔요; 4. 다식은 좀 달아요; 5. 샘과 하루는 코코넛 유과와 쌍화차를 주문했어요.

8과	Pre-reading activity	1. 게임해요; 2. 요리해요; 3. 등산해요; 4. 책을 읽어요; 5. 여행해요; 6. 유튜브를 봐요
	Reading	1. 타오 씨의 취미는 게임이에요; 2. 타오 씨는 지난주말에 롤 파크에 갔어요; 3. 롤파크는 서울에 있어요; 4. 타오 씨는 치맥을 먹었어요. 프리야 씨는 치콜을 먹었어요; 5. 타오 씨는 다음 주에 등산을 가요.
	Pre-listening activity	1 – 축하해요; 2 – 맛있어요; 3 – 새우를 못 먹어요 ㅠㅠ!
	Listening activity	A) 4; B) 1. 파전집은 진짜 맛있었어요, 2. 소피아 씨는 파전하고 떡볶이를 먹었어요, 3. 프리야 씨는 새우를 못 먹어요. 왜냐하면 알레르기가 있어요.

9과	Pre-reading activity	Purchase a ticket: 티켓 구매; modify a booking: 예약 변경; cancel a booking: 예약 취소
	Reading	2
	Listening activity	A) 4; B) 1. 이 기차는 서울에서 출발했어요; 2. 이 기차는 곧 도착해요; 3. 미리 준비해요. 그리고 가방을 꼭 가지고 내려요

10과	Pre-reading activity	육포, 막걸리, 물, 김밥, 모자, 콜라, 초콜릿, 커피믹스, 장갑, 등산 스틱
	Reading	1. 오늘 타오 씨는 등산해요; 2. 북악산은 높은 산이 아니에요. 그래서 타오 씨는 북악산을 좋아해요; 3. 타오 씨는 초콜릿, 커피믹스, 육포, 물과 수건을 가져 가요; 4. 타오 씨는 등산 사진을 인스타그램에 올릴 거예요.
	Pre-listening activity	두부집이에요; 북악산 입구에 있어요
	Listening activity	1. 프리야 씨와 친구들은 오늘 북악산 등산을 갔어요; 2. 근처 식당에 밥을 먹으러 가요. 3. 그 식당은 유명한 두부집이에요; 4. 타오 씨는 두부를 엄청 좋아해요.

Listening transcript

 ● **1-2 / Listening activity script**

공항버스 기사: 안녕하세요? 터미널 1이에요? 터미널 2예요?
타오: 안녕하세요? 저는 터미널 1이에요.
사랑: 저는 터미널 2예요.
공항버스 기사: 티켓? 신용카드예요? 현금이에요?
타오: 저는 신용카드예요.
공항버스 기사: 여기 찍으세요.
사랑: 아, 저는 현금이에요.
공항버스 기사: 잠깐만 기다리세요.

 ● **2-2 / Pre-listening activity script**

1. Passenger: 여기가 시청이에요?
   Bus driver: 아니요. 시청이 아니에요. 여기는 광화문이에요.
2. 여기에서 내리세요.
3. 다음 정류장은 뉴서울 호텔이에요.

● **2-3 / Listening activity script**

우미드: 기사님, 여기가 뉴서울 호텔이에요?
공항 버스 기사: 뉴서울 호텔이 아니에요. 여기는 서울 더 플라자 호텔이에요.
우미드: 그럼 뉴서울은 언제예요?
공항 버스 기사: 뉴서울은 다음이에요.
효과음 : bus stop (끼이익: 음성 효과)
우미드: 지금이에요?
공항 버스 기사: 네. 여기에서 내리세요.
우미드: 네. 감사합니다.

 ● **3-3 / Listening activity script**

사랑: 뭐 찾으세요?
손님: 얼음이요. 혹시 아이스컵 있어요?
사랑: 네, 있어요. 저기에 냉장고가 있어요. 거기에 있어요.
..

..

손님: 여기요.
사랑: 5천원입니다. 봉투 100원이에요. 필요하세요?
손님: 네, 감사합니다.
사랑: 감사합니다. 안녕히 가세요.

● 4-2 / Pre-listening activity script

1. 손님: 립밤 한 개 더 있어요?
   직원: 네. 잠시만요. 여기에 있어요.
2. 면도기는 네 개 있어요.

● 4-3 / Listening activity script

직원: 반갑습니다. 오늘도 올리브영입니다.
        …(잠시 후)
소피아 : 저…면도기가 어디에 있어요?
직원: 면도기요? 여기에 하나 있어요.
소피아: 감사합니다. 혹시 면도기 두 개 더 있어요?
직원: 네, 있어요. 잠시만요.
소피아: 아, 그리고 이 립밤도 세 개 주세요.
직원: 네, 알겠습니다.
소피아: 감사합니다.
직원: 감사합니다. 또 뵙겠습니다.

● 5-2 / Pre-listening activity script

1. 사랑: 기사님, 3명이에요.
   버스 기사: 잠깐만 기다리세요. 지금 카드를 대세요.
2. 캐롤라인: 한국에서 카드 1장으로 3명이 탈 수 있어요.
   소피아: 알겠어요.

● 5-3 / Listening activity script

소피아: 버스 카드가 없어요.
캐롤라인: 그럼 소피아 씨 먼저 타세요. 기사님, 2명이에요.
버스 기사: 잠깐만요. 기다리세요.
            삐삑 (소리)
버스 기사: 지금 카드를 대세요.
캐롤라인: 네.
효과음 : "삐삑 두 명입니다"
캐롤라인: 소피아 씨, 한국에서 카드 1장으로 두 사람이 탈 수 있어요.
소피아 : 알겠어요. 고마워요.
효과음: … (이번 정류장은 반포 한강공원입니다.)
캐롤라인: 여기가 반포 한강 공원이에요. 이번에 내리세요.

● 6-2 / Listening activity script

가이드: 안녕하세요?. 저는 투어 가이드 오누리예요. 만나서 반갑습니다.
        오늘 여러분들께 전쟁기념관을 설명해요. 먼저 여기 지도를 보세요. 메인 전시관은 이쪽에 있
        어요. 그리고 기념관 정문 앞에 평화 광장이 있어요. 어린이 박물관은 저쪽에 있어요. 그리고
        주차장 근처에 식당이 있어요. 거기에는 카페도 많아요.
        화장실은 주차장과 어린이 박물관 근처에 있어요. 지금까지 질문 있으세요?
캐롤라인: 기념품은 어디에서 팔아요?
가이드: 기념품은 메인 전시관 1층에서 팔아요.
캐롤라인: 네, 감사합니다.

7-2 / Listening activity script

하루: 우와 이 찻집에 한과 종류가 많아요.
캐롤라인: 네!
샘: 이건 이름이 뭐예요?
캐롤라인: 이건 약과예요.
샘: 약과 바로 위에는요?
하루: 아 그건 강정이에요. 그리고 그 옆은 유과예요. 이 찻집에서 코코넛 유과가 제일 맛있어요.
샘: 그래요? 유과 아래는요?
캐롤라인: 유과 밑에는 다식이에요.
샘: 다식이요?
캐롤라인: 네, 다식은 보통 차하고 같이 먹어요. 다식은 좀 달아요.
샘: 그럼 우리 주문해요! 저는 코코넛 유과 3개하고 쌍화차 주세요!
하루: 저도요.
캐롤라인: 저는 약과 두 개하고 아이스 시나몬 커피 주세요.

8-2 / Listening activity script

하루: 소피아 씨, 어제 생일이었어요?
소피아: 네, 그래서 어제 저녁에 생일 파티를 했어요. 그 다음에 친구들이랑 노래방에 갔어요.
하루: 와~ 생일 축하해요! 그 다음에 뭐 했어요?
소피아: 그리고 게스트하우스 근처 파전집에도 갔어요. 너무 재미있었어요.
프리야: 그 파전집은 어땠어요?
소피아: 파전이 진짜 싸고 진짜 맛있었어요. 그리고 거기에서 떡볶이도 팔아요. 근데 떡볶이도 대박 맛있었어요. 프리야 씨도 나중에 한번 가 보세요.
프리야: 파전집에서 떡볶이도 팔아요? 와~ 그런데 혹시 그 집 파전에 새우가 있어요?
하루: 네! 새우가 있어요. 왜요?
프리야: 아 저는 새우를 못 먹어요. 새우 알레르기가 있어요.

9-2 / Listening activity script

열차 안내 방송: 지금 이 기차는 서울역에서 오후 8시 30분에 출발하는 부산행 ktx입니다. 기차가 곧 출발합니다. 오늘도 ktx 기차를 이용해 주셔서 감사합니다.
  –(기차 소리)
우리 기차는 곧 부산역에 도착하겠습니다. 미리 준비해 주세요. 그리고 여러분의 가방을 꼭 가지고 내리세요. 안녕히 가세요.

10-2 / Listening activity script

프리야: 아이고, 오늘 북악산 등산 코스가 힘들었어요. 그래서 지금 엄청 배고파요.
타오: 저도요!
우미드: 한국 사람들은 등산 후에 밥을 보통 어디서 먹어요?
프리야: 아, 보통 산 아래 식당에서 많이 먹어요. 거기에 맛집이 많아요.
우미드: 그래요? 그럼 우리 이 근처 식당에 갈까요?
프리야: 네! 좋아요! 음… 저 두부집이 진짜 맛집이고 유명한 식당이에요. 저기 어때요?
타오: 오 그래요? 저 두부 엄청 좋아해요!
우미드: 저도 괜찮아요. 그럼 저기서 밥 먹을까요?
효과음: …(띠링 식당 문 여는 소리)
식당 사장님: 어서 오세요! 몇 분이세요?
프리야: 세 명이에요.

Dialogue and listening transcript translations

🎧 Conversation

Sarang: Welcome!
Tao: Is this the Sumbisori Guesthouse?
Sarang: Yes, it is! I'm Sarang, the manager.
Tao: I'm Wang Tao from China.
Sarang: Nice to meet you.
Tao: It's nice to meet you too. May I check in now?
Sarang: Yes, you can. Please show me your passport.

🎧 Listening activity

Airport bus driver: Hello, are you going to Terminal 1 or Terminal 2?
Tao: Hi, I'm headed to Terminal 1.
Sarang: I'm going to Terminal 2.
Airport bus driver: Do you have a ticket, credit card, or cash?
Tao: I have a credit card.
Airport bus driver: Please scan it here.
Sarang: Oh, I have cash.
Airport Bus Driver: Just a moment, please.

🎧 Conversation

Sarang: Hi, I'm Sarang, nice to meet you.
Priya: Ah, hello. I'm Priya. I'm from Indonesia
Tao:I'm Tao, and Priya, are you an office worker?
Priya: No, I'm not an office worker. I'm a Korean teacher. Are you Korean, Tao?
Tao: No, I'm Chinese. Sarang is Korean.
Sarang: Yes. But I'm British-Korean.

🎧 Pre-listening activity

1. Passenger: Is this City Hall?
   Bus driver: No. It's not City Hall, this is Gwanghwamun.
2. Please get off here.
3. The next stop is New Seoul Hotel.

🎧 Listening activity

Umid: Is this the New Seoul Hotel?
Airport Bus Driver: This is not the New Seoul Hotel. This is Seoul the Plaza Hotel.
Umid: Then when is the stop for the New Seoul Hotel?
Airport Bus Driver: New Seoul Hotel is next.
                    bus stop (interruption: voice effect)
Umid: Is it now?
Airport bus driver: Yes. You can get off here.
Umid: Okay. Thank you.

🎧 Conversation

Sarang: Welcome!

...

.. (Scene: the customer is wandering around, searching for something.)

...

Customer: Do you have any banana milk?
Sarang: Oh, I'm sorry. We don't have any banana milk right now.
Customer: Oh, okay. Well, do you have a boxed meal?
Sarang: Yes. I do. It's over there.
Customer: Thank you.

🎧 Listening activity

Sarang: What are you looking for?
Guest: Ice. And do you have an ice cup?
Sarang: Yes, we do. There's a refrigerator over there. It's over there.

...

Customer: Here.
Sarang:It's 5,000 won. Would you like a plastic bag for 100 won?
Customer: Yes, thank you.
Sarang: Thank you. Goodbye.

🎧 Conversation

Haru: Sofia, where are you headed?
Sophia: I'm on my way to Olive Young in Myeongdong.
Haru: Why (are you going?)
Sophia: I need to get a toothbrush and toothpaste, and the store is having a sale right now.
Haru: Oh, really? Could you grab me a men's shaving cream and three razors, please?
Sophia: Sure, no problem.
Haru: Thanks, Sophia!

🎧 Pre-listening activity

1. Customer: Do you have one more lip balm?
   Staff: Yes, just a moment; I have it right here.
2. There are four razors.

🎧 Listening activity

Staff: Nice meeting you. "This is Olive Young again today."
...(after a pause)
Sofia: Where are the razors?
Staff: Razors? They are here.
Sophia: Thank you. Do you happen to have two more razors?
Staff: Yes, I do, just a moment.
Sophia: uh, and I'd also like three of these lip balms, please.
Staff: Okay.
Sophia: Thank you.
Staff: Thank you and we'll see you again.

🎧 Conversation

Sophia: How much is one Chapagetti (Ramyeon)?
Clerk: It is 4,000 won.
Sam: How much for one Shin Ramyeon and a water?
Clerk: Shin Ramyeon is 4,000 won, and water is 1,000 won.
Sam: I'll have one Chapagetti, one Shin Ramyeon, and two bottles of water.
Clerk: Here you go, 10,000 won.
Sophia: Thank you.

...

Sophia: The Chapagetti is delicious.
Sam: Oh, the Shin Ramyeon is good, too, but it's a little spicy.

🎧 Pre-listening activity

1. Sarang: Sir, there are three of us.
   Bus driver: One moment, please. Swipe your card now.
2. Caroline: In Korea, 3 people can ride with one card.
   Sophia: I see.

🎧 Listening activity

Sophia: I don't have a bus card.
Caroline: Well, Sophia, you can get on first. Driver, there are two of us.
Bus driver: Hold on, please wait for a moment.
Beep (sound)
Bus driver: Swipe your card now.
Caroline: Yes.
"Beep, two people" (insert automated recording sound)
Caroline: Sophia, one card gets you two rides in South Korea.
Sofia: Okay, thank you.
... (This stop is Banpo Hangang Park.)
Caroline: This is Banpo Hangang Park, please get off next.
Sophia: Thank you! I'll see you at the guesthouse in the evening.

🎧 Conversation

Caroline: Gabriel, can you recommend a museum?
Gabriel: There's a war memorial in Yongsan. How about that?
Caroline: Oh, great! What are you doing at the war memorial?
Gabrielle: Oh, I go to the exhibits there.
Caroline: Wow, that's great! I love learning about Korean history.

🎧 Listening activity

Tour guide: How are you? I'm Onuri, your tour guide. It's nice to meet you. Today, I'm going to show you the War Memorial. First, look at the map here. The main exhibition hall is this way. And in front of the main entrance of the memorial, the children's museum is over there. Additionally, there's a restaurant near the parking lot, and there are many cafés. Restrooms are located near the parking lot and the children's museum. Do you have any questions so far?
Caroline: Where can I buy souvenirs?
Tour guide: Souvenirs are available on the first floor of the main exhibition centre.
Caroline: Yes, thank you.

7과

🎧 Conversation

Tao: Priya, how are you?
Priya: Hello! Tao, do you drink coffee?
Tao: No, I don't drink coffee. I drink tea. Do you like coffee, Priya?
Priya: Yes, I love ah-ah so much, so I drink five cups of ah-ah a day.
Tao: Wow! Aren't you cold?
Priya: No, I'm not cold.

🎧 Listening activity

Haru: Wow, this teahouse offers various traditional Korean sweets.
Caroline: Absolutely!
Sam: What's the name of this one?
Caroline: It's called Yakgwa.
Sam: And the one above it?
Haru: That's Gangjeong, and next to it is Yugwa. The coconut Yugwa is the best here.
Sam: Really? What about the one underneath the Yugwa?
Caroline: Below the Yugwa is Dashik.
Sam: Dashik?
Caroline: Yes, people usually enjoy them with tea. They're quite sweet.
Sam: Let's place our order! I'll get three coconut Yugwa and a Ssanghwacha!
Haru: Same for me.
Caroline: I'll have two Yakgwa and an iced cinnamon coffee.

8과

🎧 Conversation

Sophia: Tao, what did you do yesterday?
Tao: I like to play games, so yesterday I went to an e-sports stadium.
Sophia: Wow, what did you do there?
Tao: I watched the game and got the players' autographs.
Sophia: Wow! Awesome!

🎧 Listening activity

Haru: Sofia, was it your birthday yesterday?
Sophia: Yes, I had a birthday party yesterday evening, and then I went to Noraebang with my friends.
Haru: Wow, happy birthday! What did you do afterwards?
Sophia: Then we went to a pajeon restaurant near the guesthouse, which was really fun.
Priya: How was the pajeon place?
Sophia: The pajeon was really cheap and very good, and they also sell tteokbokki, which was really good. You should try it sometime, Priya.
Priya: A pajeon restaurant also sells tteokbokki? Wow. By the way, do they have shrimp in their pajeon?
Haru: Yes, they have shrimp. Why?
Priya: Oh, I can't eat shrimp. I'm allergic to it.

9과

🎧 Conversation

Sam: Hello, is this Hello Tour?
Hello Tour: Yes. How can we help you?
Sam: I... I want to change my travel dates. My reservation number is ABC.
Hello Tour: Ah, yes, when would you like to reschedule?
Sam: Is September 20th to September 23rd available?
Hello Tour: Oh, I'm sorry, there's the Busan International Film Festival in Busan during that time, so it's difficult to change the reservation.

🎧 Listening activity

Right now, this train is a KTX travelling to Busan that leaves from Seoul Station at 8:30 pm. The train is about to depart. Thank you for using the KTX trainagain today.
-(train sound)
Our train will arrive at Busan Station soon, so please be prepared, and don't forget to take your bags with you when you get off. Goodbye.

10과

🎧 Conversation

Umid: Tomorrow is the weekend; do you want to go hiking in Bukhak Mountain?
Gabriel: Oh! I'm sorry, but I'm going to Busan tomorrow.
Umid: Busan? What are you going to Busan for?
Gabriel: There's the Busan International Film Festival on in Busan right now, so I'm going to see that.
Umid: Where's Maka?
Maka: Sorry, I'm going to Jongno tomorrow for a temple stay.
Priya: Umid, I'm free tomorrow! Let's go hiking together!

🎧 Listening activity

Priya: Oh no, it was a tough hike up Bukak Mountain today, so I'm really hungry now.
Tao: Me too!
Umid: Where do people in Korea usually eat after hiking?
Priya: Oh, Koreans usually eat at the restaurant at the bottom of the mountain. There are many good restaurants there.
Umid: Really? Then why don't we go to a restaurant around here?
Priya: Yes! Okay! Um... That tofu restaurant is really good; it's a famous restaurant. How about that?
Tao: Oh really? I love tofu!
Umid: It's okay for me as well. Shall we eat there?
...(sound of restaurant door opening)
Restaurant Owner: Welcome! How many of you are here?
Priya: There are three of us.

Textbook Line-Up

"Annyeong? Hangeul!"
Korean Alphabet:
Reading and Writing

"Annyeong? Korean!" Series
Beginner   Intermediate   Advanced   Expert

Korean Textbook (Course Integration)

Starting Korean:
Basics of reading and writing.

This introductory textbook is designed for beginners to learn Hangul effectively and easily.

- -

Annyeong? Hangul! `Rel: Oct'24`

(The Korean Alphabet Book)

Korean Textbook(Including Workbook)

- Structured for all learners, form beginners starting Korean to those mastering it.
- Each volume contains 10 units and is deaigened for a 3-month curriculum(Custom curriculum available).
- Designed for self-paced learning with a systematic and gradual progression.

- -

Annyeong? Korean! Series `Seq.Rel: Dec'24`

1~3 Volumes: Beginner(CEFR: A1~A2/TOPIK: Level 1~2)
4~6 Volumes: Intermediate(CEFR: A2~B2/TOPIK: Level 2~4)
7~8 Volumes: Advanced(CEFR: B1~B2/TOPIK: Level 3~4)
9~10 Volumes: Expert(CEFR: C1/TOPIK: Level 5)

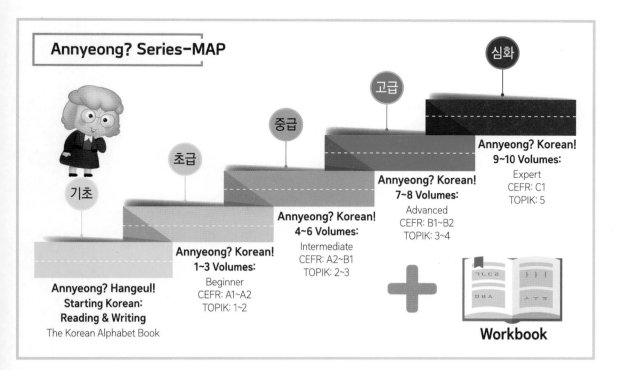

Annyeong? Series-MAP

심화

고급

중급

초급

기초

Annyeong? Hangul!
Starting Korean:
Reading & Writing
The Korean Alphabet Book

Annyeong? Korean!
1~3 Volumes:
Beginner
CEFR: A1~A2
TOPIK: 1~2

Annyeong? Korean!
4~6 Volumes:
Intermediate
CEFR: A2~B1
TOPIK: 2~3

Annyeong? Korean!
7~8 Volumes:
Advanced
CEFR: B1~B2
TOPIK: 3~4

Annyeong? Korean!
9~10 Volumes:
Expert
CEFR: C1
TOPIK: 5

+

Workbook

ANNYEONG? KOREAN! _ Volume 1

초판인쇄	**2025년 01월 02일**
초판발행	**2025년 01월 02일**
지 은 이	**조지은(Jieun Kiaer), 김현미(Hyun Mi Kim), 니콜라 프라스키니(Nicola Fraschini)**
감 수	**이인혜**
영어교정	**가브리엘 스파르타**
펴 낸 이	**허대우**
마 케 팅	**김철규 · 황현경**
편집 및 디자인	**이승미**
캐릭터 디자인	**이재엽**
펴 낸 곳	**주식회사 헬로우코리안**
주 소	**경기도 고양시 덕양구 향동로 217, 10층 KA1014호**
문 의	**hello@hellokorean.co.kr**
출판신고	**2024년 6월 28일 제395-2024-000141호**
인 쇄	**헬로우프린텍**